MICHAEL PALIN

Michael Palin established his reputation with *Monty Python's Flying Circus* and *Ripping Yarns*. His work also includes several films with Monty Python, as well as *The Missionary*, *A Private Function*, an award-winning performance as the hapless Ken in *A Fish Called Wanda*, *American Friends* and *Fierce Creatures*.

His television credits include two films for the BBC's *Great Railway Journeys*, the plays *East of Ipswich* and *Number 27*, Alan Bleasdale's *GBH*, and the three-part BBC drama, *Remember Me*.

He has written books to accompany his eight very successful travel series, *Around the World in 80 Days*, *Pole to Pole*, *Full Circle*, *Hemingway Adventure*, *Sahara*, *Himalaya*, *New Europe* and *Brazil*. He is also the author of a number of children's stories, the play *The Weekend*, and the novels *Hemingway's Chair* and *The Truth*. Michael's three volumes of diaries are *1969–1979: The Python Years*, *1980–1988: Halfway to Hollywood* and *1988–1998: Travelling to Work*.

In 2014, Michael and his fellow Pythons performed a ten-night sell-out show called *Monty Python Live* at the O2 Arena, London. Between 2009 and 2012, Michael was President of the Royal Geographical Society.

Michael Palin

MONTY PYTHON AT WORK

A behind-the-scenes account of the making of the
TV and stage shows, films, books and albums

*Selected and edited from the text of Michael Palin's published
diaries by Geoffrey Strachan*

NICK HERN BOOKS
London
www.nickhernbooks.co.uk

A NICK HERN BOOK

Monty Python at Work first published in Great Britain as a paperback original in 2014 by Nick Hern Books Limited, The Glasshouse, 49a Goldhawk Road, London W12 8QP, under licence from The Orion Publishing Group Limited

Monty Python at Work copyright © 2014 Michael Palin abridged from *Diaries 1969–1979: The Python Years* copyright © 2006 Michael Palin, and *Diaries 1980–1988: Halfway to Hollywood* copyright © 2009 Michael Palin

Copyright in the abridgement © 2014 Geoffrey Strachan

Michael Palin has asserted his moral right to be identified as the author of this work

Cover design by Katy Hepburn
Author photo by John Swannell
Typeset by Nick Hern Books, London

Printed and bound in Great Britain by T.J. International, Padstow, Cornwall

A CIP catalogue record for this book is available from the British Library

ISBN 978 1 84842 360 2

CONTENTS

PREFACE
Michael Palin

Since the publication of my diaries I've received reactions from many people in many different areas of life. Some respond to the family material, particularly those entries dealing with illness and loss. Others find particular interest in locations and shared neighbourhoods, others in political asides, still others in my involvement in transport, and trains in particular. In many ways the most surprising and gratifying response has come from writer-performers, often much younger than myself, who see in my descriptions of the agony and ecstasy of creative work, reassuring parallels in their own experience.

As diaries are about work in progress, rather than achievement explained or reputation gained, they have a directness unvarnished by time. The creation of Monty Python, through the pages of a daily diary, is a nagging reminder of the unglamorous process rather than the glamorous result. I can understand why people in the same line of work might find this helpful. I was often lifted from the gloom of elusive inspiration by reading, in her diaries, that Virginia Woolf had bad days too. Similarly, I've been told by aspiring young comedy writers and performers how encouraged they are by the travails of Python.

When my friend and scrupulous editor, Geoffrey Strachan, asked me if he could extract my Monty Python experiences from the diary into a single compact volume he made much of the fact that this could almost be an educational tool. I wasn't so sure about that. There's little point in a Do-It-Yourself Python. Monty Python is what it is and can never be recreated by following steps one, two and three. And Python is a product of its time. The way we did things will never be possible again. But the important thing is that the will to do them and the spirit that created Python is timeless. If this account of the hoops we went through to turn that spirit into reality is instructive and inspirational today then I think it will indeed have proved itself to be some sort of educational tool, albeit in a very silly syllabus.

London, January 2014

INTRODUCTION
Michael Palin

I have kept a diary, more or less continuously, since April 1969. I was twenty-five years old then, married for three years and with a six-month old son. I had been writing comedy with Terry Jones since leaving university in 1965, and, in addition to contributing material to *The Frost Report*, *Marty Feldman*, *The Two Ronnies* and anyone else who'd take us, we had written and performed two series of *Do Not Adjust Your Set* (with Eric Idle, David Jason and Denise Coffey), and six episodes of *The Complete and Utter History of Britain*. After the last one went out in early 1969, John Cleese rang me.

'Well, you won't be doing any more of those,' he predicted, accurately as it turned out, 'so why don't we think of something new.'

So it was that, quite coincidentally, Monty Python came into my life, only a month or so after the diary…

The motivation for keeping the diaries remains the same as it always was, to keep a record of how I fill the days. The perfect, well-crafted, impeccably balanced entry persistently eludes me. Prejudices bob to the surface, anger crackles, judgements fall over each other, huffing and puffing. Opinions and interpretations are impulsive, inconsistent and frequently contradictory… After all, that's where a daily diary differs from autobiography or memoir. It is an antidote to hindsight.

In the course of these diaries I grow up, my family grows up and Monty Python grows up. It was a great time to be alive.

London, January 2006

EDITORIAL NOTE
Geoffrey Strachan

During the second half of 1969, Michael Palin and Terry Jones joined forces with John Cleese, Graham Chapman, Eric Idle and Terry Gilliam to create and perform the BBC television comedy series *Monty Python's Flying Circus.* Palin and Jones had written and performed together in student revue and cabaret at Oxford University, before going on to work professionally in television comedy. Cleese, Chapman and Idle had all three had parallel experience, first in Footlights revues at Cambridge University, then with the BBC; and Terry Gilliam, an American-born artist, had done animated cartoons for London Weekend Television. Over the course of the next fourteen years, collaborating as Monty Python, they created three more television series, four cinema films, and various live stage shows in the UK, Canada and the USA, as well as five books and nine record albums. Throughout these years Michael Palin kept a diary, recording many aspects of his working, private and family life. The first two volumes of his diaries, edited by himself for publication, appeared in 2006 and 2009. Together they cover the years 1969 to 1988.

In preparing this selection from those published diaries, my intention has been to focus simply on the accounts of the working methods of the Monty Python sextet by distilling from them the passages that record scenes from the Monty Python side of Michael Palin's working life, and that of his fellow Pythons.

Readers of the complete *Diaries* will be aware that, between 1969 and 1983, Michael Palin was also involved, as writer and actor, with a great range of other television, film and book projects, notably the *Ripping Yarns* TV series and books, co-written with Terry Jones, and the film, *The Missionary*, which he also wrote and starred in. The other Pythons were similarly active. Among other things, John Cleese, with Connie Booth, wrote and starred in the TV series, *Fawlty Towers*. Terry Gilliam co-wrote and directed two films, *Jabberwocky* and *Time Bandits* (which involved Michael Palin as co-writer and actor). Eric Idle wrote *Rutland Weekend Television* (in which he starred) as well as *The Rutland Dirty Weekend Book* and a filmed Beatles spoof, *All You Need is Cash*. Graham Chapman co-wrote and starred in two films, *Yellowbeard* and *The Odd Job*, as well as writing *A Liar's Autobiography*, in which he gave his angle on Python. Terry Jones wrote several TV plays with Michael Palin, as well as their spoof children's book, *Bert Fegg's Nasty Book for Boys and Girls*, and his literary historical study, *Chaucer's Knight*.

The fact that, at irregular intervals throughout the period of their collaboration, all six of the Pythons took leave of absence from Monty Python to work on projects of their own was doubtless crucial in enabling them to come together again, as Monty Python, with renewed energy and inventiveness. The diaries show this pattern clearly. From time to time Michael Palin records that he (and the other Pythons) thought the Monty Python partnership had ground to a halt – sometimes amicably, sometimes less so. Then some inner drive, or outside circumstance, provided a trigger for work on a new project. This 'log' of the first fourteen years of their voyage together provides a record of how some of these moments looked, *at the time*, to one of the six members of this extraordinary group of writer-performers and writer directors. His diary entries give day-by-day accounts of his own involvement, and theirs, in the planning, writing, rehearsing, financing, filming, performing, editing, and – on occasion – the defence of the works of Monty Python.

In the published editions of Michael Palin's *Diaries*, he occasionally bridges a gap in continuity, or introduces a new phase in the story, with an explanatory paragraph, set in italic type. He also supplies the occasional footnote to explain a new name, as it occurs in the text. These explanatory notes and footnotes have been retained in this selection from his published *Diaries* where they occur. On the rare occasions where I have added a further explanatory note of my own, sometimes called for by a reference to a person or matter mentioned in a diary passage not here included, this has been placed between square brackets. I have also divided the book into twenty-two chapters, to assist readers in following the various, often overlapping, stages of the Pythons' progress.

I am grateful to Michael Palin and his publishers for allowing this compilation from his published *Diaries* to be presented in this form.

London, December 2013

The first BBC television series:
Monty Python's Flying Circus
(July–December 1969)

1969

I've opened the diary on the first day of Python filming. All the entries were written at my house in Oak Village, North London, except where otherwise noted.

Tuesday, July 8th

Today *Bunn Wackett Buzzard Stubble and Boot*[1] came into being, with about five minutes of film being shot around Ham House. We were filming Queen Victoria's slapstick film with Gladstone, and the beautifully kept lawn and flower beds at the back of the house provided just the right kind of formality to play off against.

In the afternoon the changes in light from sudden brightness to dullness caused us to slow down a little, but by 6.00 we had quite a chunk of 'Queen Victoria and Her Gardener' and 'Bicycle Repairman' done, and it had been a very good and encouraging first day's shooting.

Wednesday, July 9th

Arrived at TV Centre by 10.00, and was driven in a BBC car, together with John (Cleese), Graham (Chapman) and Terry (Jones),

1. The name of a fictional forward line from a John Cleese soccer monologue, and the current name for what was later to become *Monty Python's Flying Circus.* Among other titles we tried unsuccessfully to get past the BBC were 'Whither Canada', 'Ow! It's Colin Plint', 'A Horse, a Spoon and a Bucket', 'The Toad Elevating Moment', 'The Algy Banging Hour' and 'Owl Stretching Time'. Increasingly irritated, the BBC suggested the Flying Circus bit and we eventually compromised by adding the name Monty Python.

out beyond Windsor and Eton to a tiny church at Boveney. Dressed to the hilt as a young Scottish nobleman of the Walter Scott era, I was able to cash a cheque at a bank in the Uxbridge Road, without the cashier batting an eyelid.

Thursday, July 10th, Bournemouth

At Bournemouth we were met by a minivan and driven to the Durley Dean Hotel, where we were to stay that night. What with the grey weather, the lack of much to do (it was mainly Terry's 'Changing on the Beach' film) and the gradual realisation that all Bournemouth was as drab and colourless as the Durley Dean, I felt very low all morning.

After lunch we filmed on, collecting crowds of people watching Terry take his trousers down.

Friday, July 11th, Bournemouth

In the afternoon filmed some very bizarre pieces, including the death of Genghis Khan, and two men carrying a donkey past a Butlins redcoat, who later gets hit on the head with a raw chicken by a man from the previous sketch, who borrowed the chicken from a man in a suit of armour. All this we filmed in the 80° sunshine, with a small crowd of holidaymakers watching.

John, Graham, Terry and myself took a first-class compartment and talked about Shows 4 and 5 and decided that we really had an excellent week filming. Ian Mac[1] is marvellous – the best director to work for and, with a fellow Scots cameraman, Jimmy Balfour, he really gets on with it.

Wednesday, July 16th

Filming today in Barnes. The weather continues to be excellent – if anything a little too hot – 80°+ all day.

---

1. Ian MacNaughton produced and directed all the Python TV shows, apart from the first three studio recordings and a few days of film, which were directed by John Howard Davies.

Ended up the afternoon prancing about in mouse-skins for a documentary about people who like to dress up as mice. That really made the sweat pour down the chest.

Thursday, July 24th

Met with Ian and the two Terrys at the BBC. We listened to some possible title music – finally selected Sousa's march 'The Liberty Bell' from a Grenadier Guards LP. It's very difficult to associate brass-band music with any class of people. Most enthusiasts perhaps come from north of the Trent working class, but then of course it has high patrician status and support from its part in ceremonial. So in the end it is a brass-band march which we've chosen – because it creates such immediate atmosphere and rapport, without it being calculated or satirical or 'fashionable'.

Friday, August 1st

We have four shows completed, but apart from the two weeks' filming in July, there has been no feeling yet of concerted effort on behalf of the show (now, incidentally, renamed *Monty Python's Flying Circus*). However, it seems that the next two weeks will be much harder work. August 30th is our first recording date, and we have another week's filming starting on the 18th. Time is getting shorter. [Filming would be done on location, to provide scenes for insertion when the show was recorded with an audience in the studio.]

Sunday, August 3rd

John C rang up in the morning to ask if I felt like working in the afternoon, so I ended up in Knightsbridge about 3.00. It's funny, but when one has written in partnership almost exclusively for the last three years, as Terry and I have done, and I suppose John and Graham as well, it requires quite an adjustment to write with somebody different. Terry and I know each other's way of working so well now – exactly what each one does best, what each one thinks, what makes each of us laugh – that when I sat down to write with John there was a moment's awkwardness, slight embarrassment, but it soon loosened up as we embarked on a saga about Hitler (Hilter), Von

Ribbentrop (Ron Vibbentrop) and Himmler (Bimmler) being found in a seaside guest house. We do tend to laugh at the same things – and working with John is not difficult – but there are still differences in our respective ways of thinking, not about comedy necessarily, which mean perhaps that the interchange of ideas was a little more cautious than it is with Terry. However, by the time I left, at 7.15, we had almost four minutes' worth of sketch written.

Tuesday, August 5th

Another workday at Eric's.[1] A good morning, but then a rather winey lunch. That is the trouble with working at John or Eric's – both are surrounded by a very good selection of restaurants, temptingly easy to go to.

Wednesday, August 6th

Terry and I are determined to make this a really productive day. We work on till 8.00, finishing our big 'Them' saga. An 85% success day. Very satisfying – and we really worked well together.

Monday, August 18th

Started off for the TV Centre in some trepidation, for this was the first day's filming (and, in fact, the first day's working) with John Howard Davies, our producer for the first three shows. [They had already done some filming on location with Ian MacNaughton.]
John has an unfortunate manner at first – rather severe and school-prefectish – but he really means very well. He consulted us all the way along the line and took our suggestions and used nearly all of them. He also worked fast and by the end of the day we had done the entire 'Confuse-a-Cat' film, a very complicated item, and we had also finished the 'Superman' film. All this was helped by an excellent location – a back garden in a neat, tidy, completely and utterly 'tamed' piece of the Surrey countryside – Edenfield Gardens, Worcester Park.

---

1. Eric Idle.

Thursday, August 21st, Southwold

Out to Covehithe, where we filmed for most of the day. The cliffs are steep and crumbling there and the constant movement of BBC personnel up and down probably speeded coastal erosion by a good few years.

Mother and Father turned up during the morning and appeared as crowd in one of the shots.

In the afternoon heavy dark clouds came up and made filming a little slower. We ended up pushing a dummy newsreader off the harbour wall, and I had to swim out and rescue this drifting newsreader, so it could be used for another shot.

Saturday, August 23rd

In the afternoon I went over to the TV Centre for a dubbing session. Everyone was there, including Terry Gilliam, who has animated some great titles – really encouraging and just right – and Ian MacNaughton, short-haired and violent. He seems now to have dropped all diplomatic approval of John HD, and is privately cursing him to the skies for not shooting all the film he was supposed to. I think this sounds a little harsh, as the weather was twice as bad with John as with Ian.

Thursday, August 28th

This morning rehearsed [in the studio] in front of the technical boys. Not an encouraging experience. I particularly felt rather too tense whilst going through it.

Watched the final edited film for the first show. A most depressing viewing. The 'Queen Victoria' music was completely wrong, and the Lochinvar film[1] was wrong in almost every respect – editing and shooting most of all.

Terry and I both felt extremely low, but John Howard Davies, relishing, I think, the role of saviour, promised to do all he could to change the music on 'Victoria'.

---

1. John C dressed as Rob Roy is seen galloping urgently towards a church where a beautiful girl is about to be married. Cleese arrives in the nick of time – ignores the girl and carries off the bridegroom.

Saturday, August 30th

The first recording day. Fortunately Friday's fears did not show themselves, so acutely. From the start of the first run [i.e. a rehearsal on the sets] the crew were laughing heartily – the first really good reaction we've had all week. The sets were good, John kept us moving through at a brisk pace and our fears of Thursday night proved unfounded when 'Lochinvar' got a very loud laugh from the crew. In the afternoon we had two full-dress runthroughs, and still had half an hour left of studio time [before recording the show with an audience].

Barry Took[1] won the audience over with his warm-up and, at 8.10, *Monty Python's Flying Circus* was first launched on a small slice of the British public in Studio 6 at the Television Centre. The reception from the start was very good indeed, and everybody rose to it – the performances being the best ever. The stream-of-consciousness links worked well, and when, at the end, John and I had to redo a small section of two Frenchmen talking rubbish, it went even better.

The diary almost buckles under the weight of writing, filming and recording. My resolve weakens and the 1960s slip away without another entry. How could I miss the creation of the Spanish Inquisition and 'Silly Walks'? To be honest, because at the time neither I, nor any of us, I think, saw Python as a living legend, pushing back the barriers of comedy. We were lightly paid writer-performers trying to make a living in a world where Morecambe and Wise, Steptoe and Son *and* Till Death Us Do Part *were the comedy giants.* Monty Python's Flying Circus *was a fringe show, shouting from the sidelines.*

---

1. Co-writer of many shows including *Round the Horne*, father figure of Python. He pushed our series forward, and lent it an air of respectability at the BBC.

The second BBC television series;
the first film:
*And Now for Something Completely
Different*;
the first record album
(January–December 1970)

1970

Wednesday, January 14th

Since the last entry, just over four months ago, we have completed the first series – thirteen episodes of *Monty Python's Flying Circus*. The press were unanimously in praise of the show – Milton Shulman wrote a major article on it after the BBC mysteriously dropped it for two weeks after the fourth show. Jimmy Thomas of the *Daily Express* attacked *Frost on Sunday* for not realising that Monty Python had changed humour and brought it forward when Frost was trying to put it back, we have had an article in the *New York Times* and, two days ago, received the final accolade: an appearance on *Late Night Line-Up*!![1] Letters of congratulation came from Spike Milligan,[2] Humphrey Burton,[3] to name but two.

Viewing figures averaged out at three million, not bad for 11.10 on Sundays. Practical results are promises of another series, repeats of this series at a popular time, an entry for Montreux, and a possibility of a ninety-minute cinema film of the best of the series for showing in the States. This last is the pet project of Victor Lownes, London head of Playboy, who raves about the show and is, at this moment, in Chicago selling it to his boss, Hugh Hefner.

The most gratifying feature of the show's success is the way in which it has created a new viewing habit – the Sunday-night late-show. A lot of people have said how they rush home to see it – in

1. Serious BBC2 arts programme, fronted by, among others, Joan Bakewell.
2. Spike's 1969 series *Q5* had been an inspiration to us. It had been directed by Ian MacNaughton.
3. Head of Arts Programmes at BBC.

Bart's Hospital the large television room is packed – almost as if they are members of a club. The repeats – at [a more] popular time – will show us how big the club is!

Yesterday we went further into negotiations about forming Python Productions Ltd – which now seems to be decided – and next week we will set to work producing a film script for Victor Lownes.

Monday, February 16th

Somehow, since Monty Python, it has become difficult to write comedy material for more conventional shows. Monty Python spoilt us in so far as mad flights of fancy, ludicrous changes of direction, absurd premises and the complete illogicality of writing were the rule rather than the exception. The compilation of all the last series, plus new links, into the film script *And Now for Something Completely Different* has been completed, and the script should be with Roger Hancock.[1] No further news from Victor Lownes III, under whose patronage the work was done.

I am about to start writing Monty Python II, for, as Eric reminded me on the phone today, there are only eleven weeks until we go filming in May, and we are seriously intending to have eleven shows written by then.

Sunday, March 8th

We watched David Frost 'hosting' the Institute of Television and Film Arts Awards at the London Palladium. *Monty Python* was nominated for four awards and won two. A special award for the writing, production and performance of the show, and a Craft Guild Award to Terry Gilliam for graphics. But somehow the brusqueness of the programme, and its complete shifting of emphasis away from television and towards Frost and film stars, made the winning of the award quite unexciting.

None of us was invited to the awards ceremony, as the girl who was organising it 'didn't know the names of the writers' of *Monty Python.*

1. Tony Hancock's brother, who ran an agency which represented, among others, Eric Idle and Bill Oddie.

Friday, March 13th

Drove Graham down to Terry's for our first major script meeting for the next Monty Python series. At the moment we have no contract, as we are holding out for a bigger programme budget. The BBC are obviously not used to artists stipulating total budget, but it is something we feel very strongly about, and a stiff letter from Jill Foster [Michael Palin's and Terry Jones's agent] was followed by a prompt BBC offer of £4,500 per show plus £25 extra for the writers – a total increase of over £1,000 per show over the last series. (But £4,500 only makes us equal with, e.g. *World in Ferment, Charley's Grant.*) We are holding out for £5,000.

We spent most of the day reading through. Terry and I had written by far the most, and I think this may have niggled John a little.

Sunday, March 22nd

Back at TV Centre we were having an optimistic meeting with Ian M. He was sober, confident and relaxed. We talked about the BBC's idea of making an album of the best of the first series, the budget for the new series.

Thursday, April 16th

At 10.00, cars arrived to take us to the Lyceum Ballroom off the Strand to be presented with our *Weekend* TV awards. We were rushed into the stage door, where a few girls with autograph books obviously thought we were somebody, but none of them was quite sure who.

A dinner-jacketed young man with a vacant expression and an autograph book asked me if I was famous. I said no, I wasn't, but Terry Gilliam was. Gilliam signed Michael Mills'[1] name, the twit then gave the book to me saying, 'Well, could I have yours anyway?'

---

1. Michael Mills, Head of Comedy at the BBC, was the man who green-lighted Python in the summer of 1969. Despite a disastrous meeting at which we could give no satisfactory answers to any of his questions, he came out with the memorable words: 'All right, I'll give you thirteen shows, but that's all.'

So I signed 'Michael Mills' as well. We all signed 'Michael Mills' throughout the evening.

Friday, April 24th

Down at Terry's and from there to the BBC, where we all gathered to watch the playback of two of the last Monty Python series, which were being shown to an American named Dick Senior, who is interested in syndicating them in the States.

The first one we were shown was Show 11, and it was painfully slow – the 'Undertakers' and the 'World of History' were two ideas ground underfoot by heavy-handed shooting and editing and also performance. It made us look very amateur and our face was only partly saved by Show 12 – a much better-looking show with 'Hilter' and 'Upper-class Twits' providing two of the most remembered items of the series.

Dick Senior seemed a little taken aback, but he was a very intelligent man and could obviously see that there was a cumulative attraction in Monty Python, which an isolated showing could not necessarily convey.

Saturday, May 2nd

By 10.00 was at the Camden Theatre for the recording of a Monty Python LP. The original impetus for this had come from the unaptly named BBC Enterprises.

Straight away the pattern of the day was established. The record, we were told, was to be done extremely cheaply, we were not going to have it in stereo, we could not afford to pay any copyright for the use of our invaluable music links – so it was all done on an organ, which reduced everything to the level of tatty amateur dramatics.

Helped by Graham Chapman's bottle of Scotch, the actual recording, at 4.30 in the afternoon, was really quite enjoyable. Not having cameras to play to, one could judge one's audience, and one's effect on the audience, much more easily. However, the audience was small, most of the sound effects were inaudible, and we had never had time to rehearse side two, so there were many things which got little or no response – 'Hilter', 'Nudge-Nudge' and 'Soft Fruit' were especial casualties.

Monday, May 11th, Torquay

Set out for Torquay and our first two-week filming stretch away from home.

Our hotel, the Gleneagles, was a little out of Torquay, overlooking a beautiful little cove with plenty of trees around. However, Mr Sinclair, the proprietor, seemed to view us from the start as a colossal inconvenience, and when we arrived back from Brixham, at 12.30, having watched the night filming, he just stood and looked at us with a look of self-righteous resentment, of tacit accusation, that I had not seen since my father waited up for me fifteen years ago. Graham tentatively asked for a brandy – the idea was dismissed, and that night, our first in Torquay, we decided to move out of the Gleneagles.[1]

Tuesday, May 12th, Torquay

That afternoon we filmed 'Derby Council v. the All Blacks', at Torquay rugby ground, and then in the evening some night-time election sequences at a vast neoclassical mansion in Paignton, which used to belong to the sewing machine millionaire, Singer, who married Isadora Duncan. Here we filmed until midnight.

Wednesday, May 13th, Torquay

After breakfast Terry went off to film at a rubbish dump a piece of Jean-Luc Godard *cinéma-verité* involving an exploding lettuce.

We drove out to the location and spent the rest of the afternoon playing football dressed as gynaecologists.

Tuesday, May 19th, Torquay

A day on the beach. We start filming 'Scott of the Sahara', an epic film/sketch scheduled for three days. I play Scott, a sort of Kirk Douglas figure swathed in an enormous fur coat with perpetual cigar, looking more like George Burns. John plays the drunken Scottish director James McRettin, Terry plays Oates, Mike, a coloured

---

1. Eric and John decided to stay. In John's case a lucrative decision as he later based *Fawlty Towers* on Gleneagles.

ex-van-driver with a disconcerting Devonshire accent, plays Bowers, and Carol[1] plays Miss Evans. An absurd-looking bunch, we set up on Goodrington Sands, a stretch of rather stony sand south of Paignton.

Friday, May 22nd, Torquay

Today's filming, consisting mainly of short bits and pieces with the milk float ('Psychiatrists' Dairies'), had very much the end-of-term flavour.

Thursday, June 18th

To Camberwell. The morning's work interrupted by the delivery of a large amount of dung. We were sitting writing at Terry's marble-topped table under a tree sheltering us from the sun. All rather Mediterranean. Suddenly the dung-carriers appeared. Fat, ruddy-faced, highly conversational and relentlessly cheerful, they carried their steaming goodies and deposited them at the far end of Terry's garden. After about twenty-five tubfuls they were gone, but at least they left a sketch behind.[2]

Friday, June 26th

Yesterday we recorded the first of the new Monty Python series. Although there was only about fifteen minutes of studio material to record, it had gone remarkably smoothly. There were small problems during the day, but generally there was an optimistic air about the show. None of us had all that much to do, so there was perhaps less tension than usual. We even managed a complete dress-runthrough, which is almost a luxury compared to some of our hectic recordings in the last series.

The audience was full, and, even in our completely straight red-herring opening – the start of a corny pirate film which went on for nearly five minutes – there was a good deal of laughter, just in

1. Carol Cleveland, who understood the Python style so well she became almost the seventh member of the team.
2. 'Book of the Month Club Dung', which found its way into Show 6 of the second series.

anticipation. Then John's 'Hungarian Phrase Book' sketch, with exactly the right amount of lunacy and scatology, received a very good reaction.

Out to the Old Oak Common Club for a rehearsal of Show 2.

A most strange atmosphere at the rehearsal. Ian seemed a good deal less happy than last night; everyone seemed rather quiet and unenthusiastic. Perhaps it's the structure of this particular show, which consists mainly of myself as Cardinal Ximenez and Terry J and Terry G as the two other Cardinals, so the other three members of the cast have comparatively little to do.

Saturday, August 1st, Roques [Lot Valley, France]

The last recording was Show 6 on July 23rd. Eric flew to the south of France on the 24th. On that day the rest of us met Roger Hancock for lunch and formed Monty Python Productions Ltd, on the corner of Dean Street and Shaftesbury Avenue, after a convivial, but expensive and badly served meal at Quo Vadis restaurant.

Graham flew to Corfu on the Sunday morning, secure in the knowledge that his extraordinary gamble in trying to write Monty Python and thirteen Ronnie Corbett shows at the same time had been successful, for the simple reason that everyone had done the work for him on Monty Python. In fact, on Monday, when John went off to Rome, Terry and I were, as usual, left to pick up the pieces, tie up the loose ends and make sure that Ian was happy from the writing point of view before we *all* vanished.

Sunday, August 23rd

The last week has been spent filming in or around London, ending up at our traditional location – Walton-on-Thames – on Friday. It was less hot this time than in the past – I noticed this because for the last shot of the day I had to stand beside a fairly busy road clad in the It's Man[1] beard and moustache and a bikini. Next to me was John Cleese, also in a bikini.

---

1. The It's Man was a cross I'd made for myself, by suggesting that at the start of each show a haggard, wild-eyed old man should stagger out of incredibly uncomfortable situations, lurch to camera and with his last breath squeeze out the word 'It's'. I was unanimously chosen to play the part, one of the most consistently uncomfortable in Python.

Saturday, September 19th

Our running feud with the BBC Planners has come to a head, for not only is the new series going out at a time – 10.00 Tuesday – which is also the regional opt-out slot, so Wales, Scotland, Ireland, the Midlands and the South don't *see* M Python, but there is to be a break after three episodes when Python will be replaced by *Horse of the Year Show*.

Our only positive reaction in this matter was to write a very gently worded letter to Paul Fox[1] expressing our disappointment. Last Wednesday we were visited at rehearsal by Huw Wheldon, managing director of BBC TV. It was obviously a peacemaking mission. But in his favour it must be said that he *did* come, he avoided being patronising or pompous, he *had* arranged for us to see Paul Fox next week, and he *had* rung the *Radio Times* editor to ensure some more publicity.

The visit made us feel a little better and it does make us feel in quite a strong position for next week's meeting with Paul Fox.

Thursday, September 24th

At 6.30 we all trooped up to the sixth floor for our meeting with Paul Fox, Controller of Programmes, BBC1. He was clearly more nervous than we were – but then he was in a fairly indefensible position, and there *were* six of us.

Fox started by explaining why MP went out at 10.10 on a Tuesday night. Two things I felt were wrong here. One was his premise that it wasn't a pre-nine o'clock show, although I would reckon 8.30 would be its ideal time, judging from the reactions of my ten-year-old nephew, his six-year-old brother, and the large teenage section of the audience at the shows.

But Fox was conciliatory throughout. He sugared the pill with promises of a repeat of eight episodes of Series 1 immediately following our present series and, next year, a total repeat of Series 2 at a national time. He clearly realised that he had underestimated Monty Python, but his apologetic manner did encourage us to talk freely with him about some of our other complaints, e.g. lack of any

1. Controller, BBC1.

BBC publicity for the new series, the removal of our invaluable researcher, the budget (which he hotly defended as being above average for LE [Light Entertainment]: moot point) and the two-week break in our transmission after the first three shows.

Monday, October 26th

Today we started filming *And Now for Something Completely Different*. I was picked up in an enormously comfortable black Humber Imperial and driven, in the company of Graham and Terry, to our location in Holloway. It was a school gymnasium where we were filming the 'Soft Fruit' sketch,[1] but when we reached the location I felt a sudden, nervous tightening of the stomach, as I saw a line of caravans parked by the side of the road – and opposite them a large white caterer's lorry and lighting generator.

Terry and I were sharing a caravan. It was very spacious and comfortable, with a dressing room and a kitchen in it.

We were on the set by 8.30, changed and ready to film. The 35mm camera was another impressive sign that this was a film, as were the many people whose sole job seemed to be to look after us, give us calls when we were required, fetch us coffee if we wanted it, and generally keep us sweet. But our mirth was great when we saw a man struggling to stick an 'Eric Idle' sign on the back of a picnic chair. Did we really all have chairs with our name on? Yes we really did and, by the end of an eleven-and-a-half-hour day, with only a half-hour break at lunch, I realised that the caravan, the chairs and the ever-helpful production assistants were there to help us work harder, and they were vital. To have a place to relax after a take, without having to worry about finding out what is happening next, is a luxury we never had on television filming.

The crew seem, without exception, to be kind, friendly and efficient. Ian seems happy and confident, in short, it is a very enjoyable and impressive first day. We have finished the 'Soft Fruit' sketch – which is about four minutes of film.

---

1. In which John plays a crazed RSM teaching a bunch of squaddies how to defend themselves against bananas and various other forms of soft fruit.

Saturday, October 31st

We have finished a week's filming now. In retrospect, Monday was our best day in terms of output, but we filmed at a steady rate throughout the week. On Wednesday we started a week's location shooting at Black Park – an expanse of pine forest, silver-birch copses, open grassland and beech-covered lakeside, which happens to be just next door to Pinewood Studios. By Friday we had shot the 'Lumberjack Song', the 'How Not to Be Seen' opening and most of the 'Joke' film. Morale in the unit is very high.

Sunday, November 8th

After washing my hair and shaving at 7.00 in the morning, I am driven to work and immediately my hair is caked down with grease and my face given a week's growth of beard.

Ken Shabby[1] was especially revolting, with an awful open sore just below the nose. But Terry J (who has seen the rushes) is worried that it was shot with too much emphasis on Shabby and not enough wide shots to create the joke – which is the relationship of this ghastly suppurating apparition to the elegant and tasteful surroundings.

Monday, November 9th

We are filming now at the empty, recently sold A1 Dairy in Whetstone High Street.

The dairy premises are so far excellent for our sketches – for they have the same rather dreary atmosphere of failure which characters like Scribbler and Mr Anchovy and the marriage-guidance man are born from.

It takes a long time to set up the lights and to lay the track for the first shot. Once the first shot is done, progress becomes faster. From the performance point of view, I enjoy the security of being able to do a performance several times and, with the sketch actually done in sections, one is not so worried about remembering words.

1. Shabby, a disgusting man with a pet goat, who appeals to the father of a beautiful upper-class girl (Connie Booth) for her hand in marriage, but spoils his chances by, among other things, gobbing on the carpet.

Thursday, November 12th

Shooting at a pet shop in the Caledonian Road. It's a grey, wet, messy day and this particular part of the Caledonian Road is a grey, wet, messy part of the world. In the pet shop there is scarcely room to move, but the angel fish and the guppies and the parrots and the kittens and the guinea pigs seem to be unconcerned by the barrage of light – and the continuous discordant voices. The shop is still open as we rehearse. One poor customer is afraid to come in, and stands at the door, asking rather nervously for two pounds of Fido.

Friday, November 13th

A busy day filming the remains of 'Upper-class Twit of the Year' in fine, sunny weather.

Wednesday, December 9th

I wasn't required on the last day of shooting, but a car collected me in the evening and took me down to Greenwich for the end-of-film party at the Admiral Hardy. It had been a happy film, because each day made people laugh, but if it had been made in a time of full employment, when producers and production managers had to pay a crew well to keep it, our film would have been in trouble, for the relationships between the cheese-paring producers and the hardworking crew were at times near breaking point – only the precarious employment situation in the film industry kept some of the men at work.

Thursday, December 10th

Rung by the BBC and asked if I would like a three-day trip to Munich with Ian at the beginning of next week – to discuss possibility of a co-production between Monty Python and fellow funsters from Bavarian TV.

Tuesday, December 15th

In the evening we go round to Graham Chapman's for food, drink and Monty Python No. 12. It was really an evening for Python authors and their wives/lovers. The company was good and the drink was abundant, and the show – which was the first one of this new series that we recorded – had edited together well, and was especially good because of the diversity of ideas: the false 'Black Eagle' pirate opening, the dirty phrase book, the paintings going on strike in the National Gallery. Terry Gilliam's 2001-style animations, the Ypres sketch with its false starts, the overacting hospital, were just a few of them. By general consent, one of the best shows we've done.

Sunday, December 20th

I got ready for the third successive drinking evening – this time it was the BBC Light Entertainment Group who were the hosts. An article in *The Times* on December 16th had detailed, fairly promi nently, the continuing saga of Python's mistreatment by the BBC Programme Planners.

David Attenborough, who is, I believe, Assistant Controller of Programmes,[1] edged his way over to me quite early in the evening and began some rather nervously jocose banter. 'I feel I ought to come and talk to you – being one of those responsible for the repression of Monty Python.' But he made the point that the programme had done extremely well as a result of the BBC's treatment – which is an argument one cannot deny, and any altruistic feelings for the viewer in regions that don't get Python, must always be tempered with the knowledge that it's because of them we get assured repeats, and the extra loot which accompanies them.

Thursday, December 31st

Apart from some dubbing still to do on the film, Monty Python is finished – we spent almost a year on one thirteen-week series and six weeks making a film – now it remains to be discussed as to whether or when we do another series.

1. In fact, he was Director of Programmes.

Live stage show at Coventry;
the second record album:
Another Monty Python Record;
Monty Python's Big Red Book;
Bavaria Television Show in Munich;
the third BBC television series;
Lincoln Pop Festival
(January 1971–August 1972)

1971-1972

Around this time Python morphed into a stage show. Tentatively at first, but it was the start of something that was to snowball from the West End to Broadway and eventually to the Hollywood Bowl.

Sunday, January 31st, 1971, Coventry

As Terry and I walked through the deserted, rain-soaked streets of Coventry at 11.45 at night, for the first ever Python stage show, it was amazing, exciting and rather frightening to turn the corner and see the Belgrade Theatre seething with people like bees round a honeypot. There was shouting and cheering before anything had happened. There were ten men dressed as 'Gumbies' in the front row of the circle.

When, at 12.00, the house lights faded, John entered as the Spanish narrator in the 'Llama' sketch, and there was a mighty cheer and prolonged applause. As soon as Gumby came on for 'Flower Arrangement', the show ground to a halt again with almost hysterical cheering greeting each line (a good example of the 'primitive' style in comedy). For the first half of the show there was a vocal majority killing lines, laughs and all attempts at timing. After a while they seemed to tire themselves out, and one had the satisfaction of hearing people laugh at jokes and words, rather than cheering each character who came on, at random throughout the sketch.

We finished at about 1.30 a.m., but the audience refused to leave – even after the auditorium lights had been on for some time. If any of us so much as put a head around the curtain there was wild applause. After two or three minutes of this, John went out and spoke to them like the good headmaster he is – thanking them for being a wonderful audience and adding savagely: 'Now will you *please* go home.' This they enjoyed even more – and it must have been over five minutes after the end that they at last stopped applauding.

We have created characters which we ourselves find hysterical; why should we then be surprised that an audience reacts in the same way?

Friday, March 5th

In the evening, a sneak preview of *And Now for Something Completely Different*. It is on at the Granada, Harrow. We are led upstairs and seated on the left-hand side of the circle, about six rows from the front.

Then the curtains draw back, and there is our film. I found it dragged heavily, and parts of it were downright dull. But my judgement is probably coloured by seeing most of it before.

Sunday, March 14th

Python's success has resulted in a number of offers – e.g. a Python Christmas book (Methuen), three separate record contracts (Decca, Tony Stratton-Smith[1] and good old BBC Enterprises, who despite themselves appear to have sold over 10,000 of our first LP), merchandising T-shirts, West End shows for Bernard Delfont, etc., etc.

Terry and I and T Gilliam feel very much that we are in danger of losing sight of the wood for the trees. Python is a half-hour TV show and cannot easily be anything else. Any transformation of this show onto record, or onto the stage, will inevitably lose something from the original. The alternatives are therefore to put out these weaker substitute Pythons and make money from very little work, or else to work hard to make everything Python is involved in new, original, critical and silly.

We now have John Gledhill – of the Roger Hancock office – acting as the organiser and agent for Python Productions. It is going to be a hell of a job. Today we talked about notepaper!!

---

1. Racehorse owner, John Betjeman fan and general bon vivant, Tony started Charisma Records. He died, much missed by all, in 1987.

Some kind of sanity has prevailed, in that John C, after being reluctant to do any more TV Pythons, is gradually becoming one of the staunchest advocates of a new series, to be made in the autumn.

Monday, March 29th

Today, more filming for the May Day Show,[1] including one gag involving John and myself – in the Grimsby Fish-slapping dance – which ends up with my being knocked about eight feet into the cold, green, insalubrious waters of the Thames.

Wednesday, May 12th

Terry and I have been working fairly solidly together. We have been writing our Munich show,[2] which has been like old times, with lots of wild ideas developing.

On May 5th I was twenty-eight, and on May 6th at lunchtime we heard that we had come second at the Montreux Festival – winning the Silver Rose. The winner was an Austrian show, which everyone said was exactly like Python and I must say the title – 'Peter Lodynski's Flea-Market Company' – is not entirely dissimilar. But the lesson of Montreux is why did a Python copy defeat a Python original? The answer I fear is that their production and presentation was slick, whereas ours was unforgivably sloppy.

Sunday, June 20th

The first day of recording on our second LP in the Marquee Studios. It was a good feeling to be working on Sunday in the middle of Soho – and the session is run almost entirely by and for ourselves. Unlike our previous BBC record there is no audience, and we are able to do several takes on each sketch to try and improve on it. This is very

1. An attempt to produce a euro-comedy link-up to mark May Day. We were chosen to provide the British segment, for which we created a number of very silly traditional dances.
2. The brainchild of German producer and Python fan Alfred Biolek, this was to be a show written by and starring the Pythons, speaking German. It was duly recorded at Bavaria Studios in Munich in early July 1971. At least I can now sing the 'Lumberjack Song' in German – a great way of clearing crowded ski slopes.

beneficial in one way, but I shall be interested to hear whether we need the impetus of a live audience – whether in fact we subconsciously concentrate harder and bring better performances out of ourselves if we have an immediate soundboard for our antics. There is one very amenable young engineer, and Terry J is producing.

Monday, June 21st

Another day spent in the recording studio in Dean Street. We worked hard, but my doubts about the record began to grow. Firstly, because it contains fewer bankers (i.e. strong, memorable sketches) than the first record. This is partly explained by the fact that the more conventional verbal sketches translate easily onto record, whereas the more complicated, tortuously interwoven sketches of the second series lose more away from their visual context. I wish that everyone had been prepared to put some work into the writing of the record.

Wednesday, August 4th

Meeting this morning between Charisma Records and John Gledhill, Terry Gilliam and myself to discuss the record cover. Our suggestion was not the easiest thing to sell. A classical record, with everything crossed out rather crudely and 'Another Monty Python Record' scribbled in at the top. On the back a 97% authentic spiel about Beethoven and about the finer points of his Second Symphony – but, for those who can bear to read it through, it is gradually infiltrated by tennis references.

The four-month gap at this point is the result of that diarist's nightmare, the loss of an almost complete notebook. If anything, I compensated by writing more.

Tuesday, December 28th

To the Odeon Kensington to see our film *And Now for Something Completely Different*. It lasted eleven weeks at the Columbia and took nearly £50,000 at that cinema alone (over two thirds of the cost of making the picture). Its one week at Oxford ran into four weeks as a result of the demand, and it was held over for an extra week in Leicester and Liverpool. All of which bodes well for a film which Terry and I thought would be received with jeers.

Friday, December 31st

On the face of it we have achieved a lot. A TV series, which has reached the sort of national notoriety of *TW3* [*That Was the Week That Was*]. 'Monty Python', 'Silly Walks', 'And Now for Something Completely Different', etc., have become household words. The TV series has won several awards during the year, including the Silver Rose of Montreux. The second Monty Python album has sold 55,000 copies since release in October, and *Monty Python's Big Red Book* completely sold out of both printings within two weeks. It has sold 55,000 copies, and 20,000 more are being printed for February. In London it was top of the bestseller lists.

From all this no one can deny that Monty Python has been the most talked about TV show of 1971 – and here is the supreme irony, for we have not, until this month, recorded any new shows since October 1970.

The split between John and Eric and the rest of us has grown a little recently. It doesn't prevent us all from sharing – and enjoying sharing – most of our attitudes, except for attitudes to work. It's the usual story – John and Eric see Monty Python as a means to an end – money to buy freedom from work. Terry J is completely the opposite and feels that Python is an end in itself – i.e. work which he enjoys doing and which keeps him from the dangerous world of leisure. In between are Graham and myself.

Friday, January 7th, 1972

Back into our routine again – a week of dubbing, writing, rehearsing, and recording.

Today there are two major sketches – one with Graham C as Biggles, using generally abusive language, dictating a letter to King Haakon thanking him for the eels, and finding out Algy was a homosexual – the other was a parrot-shop type of sketch with John as a customer in a cheese shop, and myself as an obliging assistant, who has none of the cheeses the customer asks for – and John goes through about fifty, before shooting me. Typical of the difference in writing since the first series, is that, no longer content to just write in a cheese shop as the setting, there are throughout the sketch two city gents dancing to balalaika music in a corner of the shop. Our style of humour is becoming more *Goon Show* than revue – we have finally thrown off the formal shackles of the *Frost Report* (where we all cut our teeth), and we now miss very few chances to be illogical and confusing.

Thursday, February 3rd

After a morning's work at Camberwell, we drove over to John's for lunch and a chat about possible new additions to the cabaret at Nottingham University. We decided to put in 'Argument' sketch – a quick-fire Cleese/Chapman piece from the new series, and one or two smaller additions such as the 'Silly Ministers' and the 'Time-Check' – 'It's five past nine and nearly time for six past nine. Later on this evening it will be ten o'clock and at 10.30 we join BBC2 in time for 10.33. And don't forget tomorrow, when it'll be 9.20,' etc., etc.

Apparently the demand for tickets had been so great that we had been asked to do an extra performance, with about 700 students at each. They were a very good audience, not drunk, intelligent and appreciative. Our performances were a little edgy, as we were doing new material for the first time, but the second house – at 9.15 – was much better. We did about forty minutes each time, and were paid a little less than £200 each for the evening.

Thursday, February 10th

Assembled for an all-Python writing meeting at Terry's at 10.00. John sends word that he is ill. Extraordinarily sceptical response. However, we work on, and for a laugh decide to write a truly communal sketch. Accordingly all four of us are given a blank sheet of paper and we start to write about two exchanges each before passing on the paper. After an hour and a half we have four sketches – with some very funny characters and ideas in them. They may all work if interlocked into a four-sketch mixture.

Friday, February 11th

Drove in to Python Prods. offices to meet Alfred Biolek, here on a five-day flying visit. He told us that the show we made in Germany had been shown with generally favourable reactions, and he wanted us to fly over for a weekend and discuss plans for a second German-made programme in September.

Monday, February 14th

Drove down to Terry's and we worked at putting a show together.

Tuesday, February 15th

At 10.30 Eric arrives and we work together rewriting three film pieces of Eric's for the next six shows. (Terry is having a day at home.)

Wednesday, March 15th

At Bart's Hospital sports ground at Chislehurst we spent the day filming Pasolini's version of the Third Test Match – complete with a nude couple making love during the bowler's run-up. Two extras actually obliged with a fully naked embrace – which must be a Python 'first'. The filming went smoothly, as it has done all this week. John C hasn't been with us, as he dislikes filming so much that he had a special three-day limit written into his contract.

Thursday, March 16th

Another good day's filming, ending with a marvellously chaotic situation at a flyover building site at Denham on the A40. I was narrator in front of the camera, describing how work was going on a new eighteen-level motorway being built by characters from 'Paradise Lost'. So behind me were angels, devils, Adam and Eve, etc., etc. All around us was the deafening noise of huge bulldozers. We were trying to time the take to the moment when the largest of these mighty earth-movers came into shot. So amidst all the dirt and mud and noise you would hear Ian shouting: 'Here he comes!' Rick the camera operator shouting: 'Move your harp to the left, Graham!'

George dashing to take Adam and Eve's dressing gowns off, then the earth-mover would stop and plunge off in another direction, and all the efforts were reversed.

Thursday, April 6th

Almost two years and nine months to the day since we shot our first feet of Python TV film at Ham, we were at Windsor to shoot what is probably our last. On July 8th 1969 we started with Terry dressed as Queen Victoria, and today we finished with myself dressed as an Elizabethan.

Tuesday, April 11th

Terry and I meet Bill Borrows of the ACTT – the film technicians' union – to ask about joining as directors (for our summer film). There are few films being made in England (only eleven this year), and the union has 70% of its members unemployed. Along with many other unions it has refused to register under the government's Industrial Relations Bill, and it may go under.

So Bill Borrows was indeed pleased to see Python people. *And Now for Something Completely Different* was, after all, a very successful British film – it's breaking box-office records at a cinema in Canada even now. We were given forms to fill in, and it looks as though there will be no trouble.

Friday, May 8th

We drove to rehearsal at the new BBC Rehearsal Room in North Acton. Although in a drably industrial area – with a view from the window as depressing as that from the old London Weekend Rehearsal Rooms in Stonebridge Park – the block is well equipped and still smart.

Thursday, May 25th

The last Python TV recording for at least eighteen months. Our last show contains the 'wee-wee' wine-taster, 'Tudor Jobs' – with a long bit for myself – both sketches which John doesn't like at all, so there is a slight tenseness in the air. It's a very busy last show, with plenty for everyone to do, and only a small amount of film. A fairly smooth day's rehearsal, but it was unusual to see Duncan Wood (Head of Comedy) and Bill Cotton at our final runthrough. Apparently they later told Ian that there would have to be cuts in the show. This is the first time they've ever suggested any censorship – in what has been quite an outspoken series.

After the show there was hardly time to feel relief or regret, as Python was cleared away for maybe the last time ever.

Saturday, May 27th

In an attempt to get most of our Python work out of the way before the summer recess at the beginning of June, we worked all yesterday on material for the German show, and this morning there was still no time off, as I had to gather scripts, props, train times, etc., for our first foray into mass cabaret – at the Lincoln Pop Festival tomorrow. It is a frustrating business trying to buy simple things like vases to smash. People are so keen to sell you the unbreakable one. I hadn't the heart to tell the man who sold me on the many virtues of plastic flowers – 'they can be cleaned when they get dirty' – that all I wanted them for was to smash them with a wooden mallet.

Sunday, May 28th, Lincoln

Dawned cloudy and grey yet again. But at least the high winds of the past two days have gone.

At about 4.00 we set out for Bardney, about ten miles east of Lincoln, and the Open-air Pop Festival (the first to be staged in England since the Isle of Wight in 1971). The first evidence of this mighty gathering, estimated at 50,000 people, was a long traffic jam stretching from the village of Bardney. People later confirmed that the jams were caused by sightseers who had come to 'look at the festival'. Most of the audience clearly couldn't afford cars.

It was about 10.45 when we embarked on what was certainly the most spectacular cabaret I've ever done. They started with our signature tune, and there was a roar of recognition from the audience. The lights were very bright, so one couldn't really see the audience, and it was difficult to judge the laughs, which came as a distant rumble – like the beginning of an avalanche. There seemed to be more people on the stage behind us than the entire audience we usually get at cabarets. I had the feeling that we had a certain interest above those of the other groups because revue has never really been attempted on this scale before. On either side of the stage were 60 x 40-foot Eidiphor[1] screens with TV pictures of our faces, and the sound was very good. We tried some new material from the third series – and one of the sketches, the 'Proust competition', lay there. Otherwise the response was pretty good, and 'Pet Shop' went tremendously well – with great surges of laughter.

Wednesday, August 2nd

John Gledhill phones with news of the advent of Python in the States. The first commercial manifestation has been the recent release by Buddah Records of our second LP, *Another Monty Python Record.*

1. Large-screen television projector devised by Dr Fritz Fischer. Last used in 2000. From the Greek *eido*; image and *phor*; phosphor/light-bearer.

The third record album:
Monty Python's Previous Record;
the second Munich show
(September 1972–January 1973)

1972-1973

Monday, September 4th

Python reassembled at Terry's after three months off. Everyone seemed happy to be starting again.

A cautionary visit from John Gledhill in the late afternoon. He brought us the latest figures for the film. Up to about five months from its release the net take (after Columbia had creamed off their share) was only $227,000. We do not start to make a penny until it has passed $500,000 and even if it took $1 million, we would still only stand to make £2,000 each. So the film, which John G reckoned had made us into world stars, has still only brought us £1,000 each. This had an amazing effect on the Python group. Suddenly everyone wanted to work. Within half an hour we had agreed on a third LP for the Christmas market, another book for next year, and a film script as soon as possible.

Thursday, September 14th

A week of great activity. In five days we have assembled a third Python LP to be in the shops for Christmas. Over half the fifty to sixty minutes' worth of material is new, and, unlike the second LP, everyone has contributed to the writing. Among the new ideas for the record were a B-side consisting of four concentric tracks, all starting at different places on the first groove, so that the listener could get any one of four different versions of the B-side; also there was an idea for an extra-large record cover, two foot square; a 'free' 'Teach Yourself Heath' record included in the LP, which would use

36

actual Heath speeches to analyse his voice, and teach people the best way of reproducing it. The title we settled on was 'A Previous Monty Python Record'.

We met for lunch and a final readthrough of material and, at 5.30, André,[1] the engineer who is doing our new LP, came round and we spent a couple of hours going through the script for sound effects and music cues. Fred Tomlinson and his singers[2] and Neil Innes, ex of the Bonzos [the anarchic Bonzo Dog Doo-Dah Band had appeared with Palin, Jones and Idle in *Do Not Adjust Your Set*], had to be contacted about music – but by 8.00 last night the material was in typeable shape and ready to be sent off to John Gledhill.

Friday, September 15th, Munich[3]

As we expected, this year was more businesslike – we spent the afternoon in costume fittings, and it wasn't until the evening that we had time to relax. Alfred (Biolek, our German producer) and Ian had fallen out for some reason, which is not a good start.

Wednesday, September 20th, Hohenschwangau

Filming in Neuschwanstein Castle. A clear and sunny day. In the distance the sun picks out the snow on the mountains of the Austrian Alps. It's a perfect day for throwing a dummy of John Cleese from the 100ft tower of the castle to the courtyard below.

I was playing Prince Walter, described in the script as 'rather thin and weedy with a long pointed nose, spots, and nasty unpolished plywood teeth'. The make-up man, George, made a superb job of personifying this creature. My own hair was laboriously curled with hot tongs into a silly little fringe, which made me look like an underfed Henry V.

---

1. André Jacquemin had engineered several sessions with me, going back to 1966. His committed, efficient, no-nonsense skills impressed me and he became Python's engineer of choice.
2. The Fred Tomlinson singers had played, among other things, the original Mounties in 'Lumberjack Song' and the original Vikings singing 'Spam! Wonderful Spam!'
3. Where we were to be based for the second of two Python specials made for Bavarian TV.

A perfect Gothic horror evening – a cool breeze, and a full moon, glimpsed through the trees and occasionally blotted out by scudding clouds. Ludicrously clad, wearing a silly false nose and carrying a crate of beer for the unit's supper, I was led through echoing passages and through stone-vaulted halls towards the filming.

Friday, September 29th, Munich

Only last night did I learn for certain that today we were to do the most complicated sketch of all – the 'Hearing-Aid' sketch. We could only use the shop to do it in after 8.00, so it was a most uneven and awkward day. As we rehearsed Ian took a phone call from his PA in England. She had received a note from Duncan Wood in which he ordered another round of cuts in the current *Python* series.

Terry J sees it as part of a plot to keep the BBC out of any major controversies until the charter has been renewed in 1974. Ian MacNaughton feels that he will be out soon anyway, as the LE bosses hardly talk to him now, and he is prepared to fight with us against this decision. Maybe we cannot win, but I feel it is as important as anything not to lie down and accept this censorship. John C, for the record, wants to avoid any confrontation with Bill Cotton and Duncan Wood.

Thomas[1] came in later on in the rehearsal and added to our increasing feeling of paranoia by telling us that Hans Gottchild, the enormous, Hemingway-bearded head of Bavaria TV, had been most displeased with the Python rushes, calling them 'dilettante'.

By the time we had filmed as coal miners at the full-scale model of a coalface in the Deutsches Museum, I felt quite exhausted. As it turned out the evening was not too bad. We worked in long takes, which required great concentration, but made the whole process seem faster. It was about 10.45 that John and I ended the sketch by hurling ourselves out of a very expensive Munich optician's, onto a pile of rugs and cushions.

1. Thomas Woitkewitsch, translator of the Python German shows.

Friday, October 27th

An eventful day. Began with a Python meeting at John's to discuss future long-term plans. An interesting thing happened. I had originally told Charisma that we did not want individual writing credits for the two sides of the single ('Eric the Half-Bee' by Eric and John and 'Yangtse Song' by myself and Terry) on the grounds that Python had never before singled out writers' specific contributions. But Eric had told Jim that he wanted his name on the single. So this was the first awkward point that I brought up with John and Eric this morning. Predictably Eric bristled, but with a bitterness that I didn't expect. He wanted his name on the record because he was going to write more songs, and this would help him. John, however, agreed with me – that the principle of Python's 'collective responsibility' was more important. But as suddenly as the storm broke it was over. Eric apologised, said I was absolutely right and that he was being stupid about it – but all this came out in such a way that I felt a warm flood of friendship as well as considerable relief.

After the meeting we all drove over to the BBC to see Duncan Wood and discuss the cuts he proposed in our new series. These cuts involved the excision of whole sketches about a French wine-taster who serves his clients only wee-wee, and an awful City cocktail bar where upper-class twits ask for strange cocktails – one of which, a mallard fizz, involves cutting the head off a live duck. Other cuts included the word 'masturbating' (a contestant in a quiz game gives his hobbies as 'golf, strangling animals and masturbating'), the phrase 'I'm getting pissed tonight' and most of two sketches, one about a dirty vicar and the other about the Oscar Wilde Café Royal set, who run short of repartee and at one point liken King Edward VII to a stream of bat's piss. But we were protesting mainly about the volume of the cuts, not particular instances. Our point was basically why, if we are going out at 10.15 – well after children and family peak viewing – are we suddenly being so heavily censored?

Duncan Wood at first protested that we weren't being heavily censored, that four cuts in the first nine shows wasn't bad. (I must say in the first of the series we got away with the line from a judge, 'Screw the Bible, I've got a gay-lib meeting at 6.00,' which certainly couldn't be spoken on any other TV service in the world.) So he has clearly relented over certain of the cuts he wanted Ian to make. He promised to review Shows 12 and 13 again, with us, so that we could all see what we were talking about.

We got to talking about censorship generally – and why the BBC seemed to be suddenly more frightened of causing offence. Genial Duncan chain-smoked and talked in a vague and roundabout way of 'pressures from outside' causing a temporary tighten-up in censorship. There seemed no evidence that there was popular support for BBC censorship – quite the opposite – the most outspoken of BBC progs, *Till Death Us Do Part*, has an audience of nearly 20 million, and Python itself has higher viewing figures than ever (round about 10 million for the first show of the latest series).

Saturday, November 4th

Spent three hours with André, editing and tightening the B-side of the new album until it was in a very strong and satisfying shape, then, with Terry and André, walked across Regent Street and into Savile Row, where the Apple Studios are situated in a well-preserved row of Georgian town houses. They seem to be the only place that has the technology to cut our multiple B-side.

At one point, about 7.00, I had just come back into the studios after having a drink when a slight, thin figure walked towards me. The face was familiar, but, before I could register anything, a look of recognition crossed George Harrison's face, and he shook my hand, and went into a paean of praise for Monty Python. He said he couldn't wait to see Python on 35mm, big screen.

Finally left Apple about 8.00 – the cutter, John, promised to have more attempts at the cut over the weekend, but the chances of producing this highly original B-side don't seem too rosy.

Tuesday, November 7th

Heard during the afternoon that Apple were unable to cut the three-track B-side [originally planned with four tracks]. Terry took the tapes round to EMI for them to have a go, so we can only cross our fingers.

Wednesday, November 8th

EMI cannot do the cut, what shall we do? Almost an hour is spent ringing round the Pythons to get them to a meeting on Thursday to listen to the record. We decide to cut the B-side in mono, which apparently will allow the three-track cut to work. So Apple now have the job again.

Monday, December 4th

A very successful Python meeting at John's. Everyone was remarkably direct about future plans and there was a remarkable freedom of pressure on anyone to fit in with others' plans. The basic factor in the future life of Python is that John has had enough of Python TV shows – he doesn't enjoy writing or performing them and will not commit himself to any more Python work after the film next summer.

The next major factor was that Eric and Graham especially were concerned about making some money next year. To solve this we decided to try and fix up a two- or three-week university tour in April, on the lines of our successful Coventry Festival show a couple of years ago.

Later in the evening, Eric rang me up – still a little worried about where work, therefore loot, was to come from in the next year. I had mentioned my keenness to do some more TV next Christmas and Eric was ringing to lend support to this. Has today seen the first seeds of a new post-Python TV series without John and possibly without Graham [sown], or will we, as I forecast, find ourselves all together again next December?

Thursday, December 7th

At 12.30 arrived at TV Centre to see a playback of our controversial Shows 12 and 13, which Duncan Wood and Bill Cotton have told us must be amalgamated into one, on the grounds of their (to them) offensive tastelessness. We had asked at least if we could see again what we were being accused of, and we had asked that Paul Fox might view the shows as well.

This he was doing in an upper room of the BBC at the same time as we were seeing them in a lower room. Both shows had generally scatological themes, but in nearly every case the naughty material was hardly worth making a fuss about, and most of it was less questionable than some of the material in the first two series (viz. the mother-eating sketch). Neither show was our best, but I certainly could see no earthly reason for combining the two and wasting an entire show.

That evening I was very glad to hear from Ian that Fox had felt this way too, and had insisted on far fewer cuts than Wood and Cotton. This was the first time we have ever divided the BBC hierarchy.

Monday, January 1st, 1973

A good start to the New Year – Python has won the Critics' Circle Award as the best comedy show of the year.

The first live road tour;
writing the second film:
Monty Python and the Holy Grail;
live stage tour of Canada;
publicity on US television
(January–June 1973)

1973

Thursday, January 25th

Met Tony Smith[1] – the man who is probably going to land the first ever Python road tour... He was quietly confident that a Python tour would be a sell-out. Bannister Promotions have offered us a guarantee of £17,500, but Tony Smith reckons that we could make 21 or 22 grand – on a percentage split with him. Smith has fairly impressive credentials, including recent sell-out tours with The Who and Led Zeppelin.

Saturday, January 27th

At 2.00 we had a Python meeting at John's. We decide to do the Python tour with Tony Smith. We talk about details of perform-ance and dates and places. I find it extraordinary that John can undertake such a violent month of really hard work repeating basically old material – and yet will not countenance doing another series of Python. I suppose it's all a question of time and money.

Friday, February 9th

Arrived at Rules (restaurant) about 1.00. In an upstairs room the Pythons, and several people from Methuen who had worked on the book (*Monty Python's Big Red*). On the table were individual sugar

---

1. Not to be confused with Tony Stratton-Smith, whose Charisma label put out our albums.

Gumbies, and a large chocolate 'Spiny Norman',[1] and menus on which each dish was followed by an appropriate review of the *Big Red Book* – trout followed by 'flat, thin and silly', etc. The meal was to celebrate sales of over 100,000 paperbacks.

Thursday, March 1st

In the afternoon we went to see Mark Shivas at the BBC. Talking of the future, he showed considerable interest in the Pythons' second film – and suggested a man called David Puttnam[2] as a source of money. Terry afterwards thought Shivas himself might have been interested in the producer's job.

Monday, March 5th

A Python meeting at Terry's. The first time since the third LP in September that we have all contributed to a creative enterprise – in this case the second Python film. For me, the most heartening thing of all was the quality and quantity of the writing that Python has done over the last week. John and Graham, writing together apparently untraumatically for once, had produced some very funny material. Eric had a richer selection of ideas – which sparked off a lot of other ideas, and Terry and I had a ragbag of sketches – more than anyone else, as usual, but with a pretty high acceptance rate. Today we proved that Python can still be as fresh as three years ago, and more prolific.

Friday, March 23rd

We have been working for three days on the Python film script with maximum productivity. Ideas have been pouring out, and we have had very concentrated, but quite tiring writing sessions.

---

1. Mr Gumby wore knotted handkerchiefs on his head and shouted very loudly. Spiny Norman was the giant hedgehog which the gangster Dinsdale Piranha was convinced was watching him.
2. Produced *Chariots of Fire*, *The Killing Fields* and *Local Hero*, but his only major credit at this time was *That'll Be the Day* with David Essex.

Monday, April 16th

Over to B&C Records to talk about promotional work for the tour. On the steps of B&C met the beaming and effusive Tony Stratton-Smith. He has, almost single-handedly, secured Python's first TV foothold in the US – a deal with the Eastern Educational Network to put out the shows, uncut and unabridged. It's not a lucrative deal, but it's a great breakthrough. Tony now has to get two sponsors for the show and has high hopes of Apple, the Beatles' company – George H is very interested.[1]

Back home to write some programme copy for the stage tour. Helen [Michael's wife] had a good suggestion yesterday. All its pages will be on one big sheet, which can be folded up into a programme, or kept as a poster. Good Python thinking.

Easter Monday, April 23rd

The first official day of the 'First Farewell Tour', but Terry G, Terry J and myself have been working hard on it for about two weeks, collecting the film, writing and creating the programme, making slides, organising the sound tape with André.

Rehearsals started at 9.30 at the Rainbow Theatre in Finsbury Park. It's a mammoth 3,500-seater theatre, with wildly flamboyant interior.

Friday, April 27th, Southampton

We walked to the theatre. In the distance we could see the enormous liners in the docks, and some way ahead, the steel letters on a grid high above the surrounding buildings read 'Gaumont'. Altogether rather an epic place to start the tour.

The sound is clearly going to be a difficult problem, for, in addition to music and sound fx on tape (now being worked by André), we have film and animation sound from the projector, voice-overs from two offstage mics and six radio mics, all to be mixed and controlled by Dave Jacobs, a short, grey-eyed young guy, who has had about six hours' sleep in the last three days. In fact, everyone looks tired, but the adrenaline of an imminent first night keeps everyone going. By 6.00 Graham was very drunk.

1. In the end, Dusty Springfield sponsored us.

The first house was just over half-full and was happy, rather than ecstatic. But it certainly couldn't be compared with the reception we'd had at Coventry. Perhaps most amazingly of all, 'Silly Walks' went by with an almost embarrassing lack of response, and there were many cases of mics not being switched up, etc., etc. There was only half an hour before the next house, so there was only time for a cup of tea and a sandwich before we gathered on stage for 'Llamas'. John, Eric, Terry G, Terry J and Neil Innes resplendent in their Spanish gear, Carol Cleveland in her sequinned leotard, and me in an old mac with 'Eat More Pork' written on the back, and my Gumby gear underneath.

As soon as the curtain went up for the second house, the atmosphere was one of wild enthusiasm. Favourite characters – John in the 'Llama' sketch, Gumby, Terry and Graham as Pepperpots, Eric as Nudge Nudge, and Graham's Colonel and Ken Shabby – were given rounds of applause, and 'Pet Shop' at the end was as self-indulgent in performance, and as hugely popular in reception as it has ever been.

But Graham was far gone. He had missed his entrance in 'Argument' twice, made 'Custard Pie' a dull shadow of its former self, and slowed down many a sketch. Only his own 'Wrestling' had been done really well.

Later Graham, Eric and John had 'full and frank discussions', in which John told Graham straight out that he had performed very badly in both shows and if he went on like this every night there was no point in him continuing on the tour. For my own part, I feel that Graham's condition was the result of a colossal overcompensation for first-night nerves.

Saturday, May 5th, Birmingham

The tour is now in its second week, and we have done eleven shows already. My voice is getting a little husky, and I hope that if I treat it carefully it will last tonight's show at the Hippodrome and three shows in Bristol before two days off in London.

Friday, May 18th, Edinburgh

Neil and Eric very pissed tonight on stage. The unusual spectacle of Eric not quite in control. The difference in his timing showed how crucial timing is. Both his long travel-agent monologue and

'Nudge-Nudge', which usually provoke enormous reaction, went by almost unnoticed.

Sunday, May 20th, Edinburgh

The second house at Glasgow earlier in the day, was, I think, the best performance of the tour so far. Even the police had come in to watch us. Five or six of them, including two policewomen, sat behind stage and watched the second show. They managed to find a bottle of whisky for Graham from nowhere.[1] In fact, as they left, they asked us if we wanted 'anything else'.

Wednesday, May 23rd

After Leeds a long run down to Norwich, which was our thirty-fourth performance since we started at the Gaumont, Southampton, twenty-seven days before.

The first Python stage appearances abroad were on an eccentric tour of Canada. All of the team were there, augmented by Neil Innes and Carol Cleveland.

Wednesday, June 6th, Toronto

I was called at 6.30 to go for an early-show interview with CTV – the main alternative channel to CBC. Terry J and Terry G were the only other two whom Tony (Smith) could persuade to do it. Our interviewer was called Percy. As he was in a single shot doing an introduction to camera about how brilliantly zany we all were, I pointed my finger at his speaking mouth, and he bit the end of it. We talked seriously for a moment, then anarchy would break loose. He rugby-tackled Terry Gilliam as we upturned the table on set and the show ended with a chase.

Friday, June 8th, Montreal

The performance tonight, at the vast impressive Place des Arts, was nearly sold out – almost 2,500 people there, which I think is the

1. At that time Glasgow was a dry city on Sundays.

biggest crowd we've played to on the tour. Mind you, we need them – for with the expenses of hotels, etc., we stand to make little more than £1,000 each for this whole Canadian effort. (John G had once estimated it as high as £3,000 each.) However, a good audience.

Sunday, June 10th, Ottawa

Talked over the subject of the moment – whether or not to extend our tour to make TV appearances in the States. This was first mooted in Montreal by Nancy Lewis, from Buddah Records in New York, who have been responsible for a great deal of Python promotion in the States and who, apart from the record, are also trying to persuade Columbia to take the wraps off our film. Nancy, who is a very kind, gentle girl, has absolute faith in Monty Python's saleability in the States, and she has fixed up a series of TV interviews. But these will involve staying on in North America for about five days longer. John C and I are very much against this.

As I thought about it, and as I talked to Nancy, who has almost put her job in jeopardy on our behalf (for Buddah are to pay all expenses), the more I realised that I ought to go, for Python's work is not down to one person.

Monday, June 11th, Ottawa–Calgary

On the journey I started talking about Python, the States and the group itself to Graham, and it suddenly became very clear to us that if we all, apart from John, wanted to do another Python series, then we should do one. Maybe a fourth Python series was born as we flew over the wheatlands of Saskatchewan.

Wednesday, June 20th, Vancouver

Tonight, we perform 'Monty Python's First Farewell Tour' for the forty-ninth and last time. Vancouver has treated us well, with the most extensive publicity coverage so far in Canada, and, in a 3,000-seat theatre, one 70% house on Monday, over 80% on Tuesday and tonight a complete sell-out, with people turned away.

Monday, June 25th, Los Angeles

At 2.30 three of the production team of the *Midnight Special* arrived to talk over our spot in the show tomorrow night. They were very American, all slightly paunchy, and wisecracking a lot – but genially. We talked over our prepared programme, which included animation, 'Gumby Flower Arranging', a clip from the 'Silly Olympics' film, 'Nudge-Nudge', 'Children's Story', 'Wrestling' and Neil's 'Big Boots'.

Tuesday, June 26th, Los Angeles

At 5.00 we arrived at NBC Burbank Studios to record our eight-minute slot for the *Midnight Special*. There is an informal live audience, who sit around on cushions, and look modish – a cross between campus and St Tropez. A friendly, but not ecstatic reaction.

Wednesday, June 27th, Los Angeles

At 2.30 we once again drove out on the Hollywood Freeway to the NBC Studios. Whereas the *Midnight Special* has an audience more likely to appreciate Python, the *Tonight Show* is an all-American institution.

To make things more nerve-racking, it was to be recorded as a live show, with no stops or retakes, for the tape had to be ready an hour or so after recording to be flown to the various parts of the States for transmission the next evening.

A great air of unreality. Here was Python going out to its greatest single audience ever, and to us it was no more than a hastily organised cabaret. At 6.00 the recording started. This week Joey Bishop, one of F Sinatra's and D Martin's buddies, was hosting the show. Bishop was on good form, fluent and funny. When it came to our spot he produced our two latest LPs and tried, quite amusingly, to explain the crossed-out Beethoven cover. All good publicity. The sketches went smoothly – though our starter, the two Pepperpots[1] talking about soiled budgies, was totally lost.

---

1. Pepperpots was the generic name for the screechy ladies in *Monty Python*. John and Graham coined the name because of their shape.

Plans for a fourth TV series;
the second book:
The Brand New Monty Python Bok;
writing *Monty Python and the Holy Grail*;
the fourth record album:
*The Monty Python Matching Tie and
Handkerchief*;
live stage show at Drury Lane
(August 1973–April 1974)

1973-1974

Friday, August 10th

To the BBC for a meeting with Cotton and Duncan Wood about the future of Python. Cotton restated his position that if we were to do a show without John it should not be called Monty Python – it should try and be something different, and it should be tried out in an on-air pilot, with a possible series next year. We in turn had bristled at the idea of having to prove ourselves in a pilot, and so it devolved on John C.

Wednesday, August 22nd

John is clearly determined to remain uninvolved in any major Python TV project. He says he is writing with Connie, which is something he always wanted to do, and which gives him the afternoons free! He was keen on doing another record and on being involved in the next Python film.

Monday, September 10th

In the evening I spent nearly an hour on the phone with J Cleese. I feel John wants to get completely out of all Python involvement. What a long way we've come since John's phone calls four and a half years ago when he was trying to set up Python.

Thursday, September 13th

In the afternoon Terry came here. He thought of *The Monty Python Matching Tie and Handkerchief* as a title for the new LP.

Optimistic developments today – it's rumoured that the BBC will offer us seven Python shows next year.

Wednesday, September 19th

Lunchtime meeting at Methuen to discuss promotion of the *Brand New Bok*. Advance sales have already totalled 105,000, and the book isn't out until Nov 1st. There were copies there for all of us. I was pleased with the way it looked – once again the artefact had exalted the material, and I was relieved that the vast amount of sexual content in the writing was arranged so that the book didn't appear totally one-track minded.

One of the great satisfactions of the book was the success of the lifelike dirty fingerprints printed on every dust jacket. Our publisher Geoffrey Strachan told the story of an elderly lady bookseller from Newbury who refused to believe the fingerprints were put there deliberately. 'In that case I shall sell the books without their jackets,' she said and slammed the phone down so quickly that Geoffrey was unable to warn her that beneath each dust cover was a mock soft-core magazine, featuring lots of bare-bottomed ladies beneath the title: 'Tits and Bums. A Weekly Look at Church Architecture'.

Saturday, September 22nd

A big readthrough of material for the new album. A sketch which Graham and I collaborated on yesterday has John and Eric in stitches. But still nothing very exciting. One section of a 'Phone-In' type sketch, which Terry and I wrote, is about the only piece that has everyone rolling about.

Tensions flare at the end of the meeting when Terry, in passing, mentions that Mark Forstater will be fulfilling a kind of producer's function on the film – John reacts strongly, 'Who is this Mark Forstater?' etc., etc.[1] John has a way of making it sound like a headmaster being crossed by a junior pupil, rather than equal partners in a business disagreeing.

---

1. Mark Forstater, an American film producer living in London, originally introduced to us by Terry Gilliam.

Wednesday, September 26th

Terry and I went up to The Flask in Hampstead and had a good air-clearing talk about the future. We both feel now that another series of Python for the BBC – with John writing a regulation three-and-a-half minutes per show – is not worth doing, certainly at present, if at all. I was not encouraged enough by the material we wrote for the record to believe that Python has vast untapped resources. Python it seems is being forced to continue, rather than continuing from the genuine enthusiasm, and excitement of the six people who created it.

Monday, October 1st

Drove up to André's to listen to the tapes of the LP. Some sounded very flat. Terry G, Terry J and myself discuss possibility of an extraneous sound effect running throughout the record (e.g. Indian attacks or a cleaning lady using carpet sweeper, etc.) – which could be faded up to enliven some of the less exciting sketches.

Tuesday, October 23rd

At 5.00 into a quite eventful Python meeting. Everybody is present, though Graham's about half an hour late. This is the second of our 'chase Gledhill' meetings. Gledhill looks more relaxed and cooler than when I saw him at his Barbican flat a week ago. He takes control from the start, and offers for discussion a number of fairly unimportant points.

Having cleared these out of the way there is discussion about the (Michael) Codron[1] offer of six weeks, starting at Christmas, in the Comedy Theatre. Eric and John are very keen. Terry G less keen, myself very anti. For some reason I find myself in the rare position of being out on my own (though Terry J, I think, feels the same, but is keeping tactfully quiet to avoid accusations of a block vote). Briefly I see it as six more weeks of a show which I find very dull, and here

---

1. Successful West End producer for, among others, Michael Frayn, Harold Pinter, Simon Gray and Alan Ayckbourn. Gave me my first and last West End break in the Oxford Experimental Theatre production of *Hang Down Your Head and Die*, in 1964 when I was twenty-one.

we are going to the West End, forsaking our Rainbow/pop following – which, John says, 'scares the shit out of me' – for the £2.50
circle and front stalls audience, with a show that seems to me full of
old material – some of it done in the West End before. What has
become of Python the innovator?

Graham arrives, I think a little fortified. He says we have asked
for the accounts for long enough, and John has done nothing – but
John G produces an envelope and, with a triumphant smile, reveals
– six copies of the company accounts. John G follows this up with
optimistic details of payments to come within the month. Such is
the success of this move, that he manages to get away with the
extraordinary revelation that Tony Stratton-Smith does not have the
money for the film. Then I notice the beautifully presented accounts
are only for the year up to October 1971! They are two years behind.
Gilliam rants and raves and expresses his frustration very forcibly,
banging the chair. Eric is very quiet. John C wades in, though not
ruthlessly. I try to tell John G why we are dissatisfied – that he has
for too long been giving us definite optimistic pronouncements
which turn out to mean nothing. Graham gets very angry again, and
John G reacts – cleverly, in retrospect – with injured aggression. He
fights back. 'Then why not get yourself another Python manager?'
he says, sweeping his glasses off with a flourish. You could have
heard a pin drop in Waterloo Place this uncommonly mild October
afternoon. John G, unconfronted by a barrage of protests, moves
quickly on, but into an area where, for the first time he commits
himself too far – 'Frankly as far as I am concerned, Python may not
be here next year and I've got other eggs in the basket which I have
to develop as well...' He retracts and returns to safer ground, 'In any
case, I think this is the only area where I may not have produced the
goods.' Here followed the most damning silence of all.

I left the meeting feeling pleased with myself for not giving in over
the stage show, but with the unhappy feeling that somehow we must
do something for the sake of the group. As Terry G says, there is a danger that we should become too purist, and in rejecting everything
because it isn't *quite* right, we end up with nothing but principles.

Thursday, October 25th

To the office of Michael White in Duke Street, St James's. A successful and fairly prestigious young impresario.

John Goldstone[1] was there and Mark (Forstater). He and Goldstone seemed to share many of our feelings about what the film should be like. White talked of the 'really good comedy film' which has yet to be made. [The first film had been a compilation of sketches from the TV series.] What he meant was, I think, that our film should not depend on TV for anything more than a sales impetus; it should be a film of merit in itself. Such intelligent interest in our film we haven't encountered before.

Tuesday, October 30th

Tonight a long phone call from John Cleese. He proposed asking John Goldstone to our Python meeting on Thursday to explain the deal and tell us where and if he thought Mark would fit in. In the end we agreed to ask Mark along first, just to give him a hearing.

Wednesday, October 31st

John Gledhill rang this evening. I told him we were meeting Mark tomorrow. He was taken aback, but recovered. 'He's no negotiator, anyway,' says John. Finally he says, of course, whatever Mark's function, he, Gledhill, will do all the deals. I ring Mark later. Mark wants to do all the deals because he says that Gledhill is very bad at it – and was embarrassing at a meeting with Goldstone recently. Cooperation, as an option, seems to be receding. It's all a long way from being out there filming, and I find it depressing to have to get into this personal tangle. Especially as there is no villain of the piece, no easy target whom we can slander and malign. Both Gledhill and Mark are nice people.

1. John Goldstone was a film producer brought in by Michael White. I'd first met him at Barry Took's in the days before Python.

Thursday, November 1st

Surprise, surprise. A cordial, relaxed, totally constructive meeting at John [Cleese]'s. All of us present, and Mark as well. Mark explained the film deal, thoroughly and efficiently, and also gave us a run-down on how he would hope to be involved in the film, and now much of a cut he would like.

At 6.00 a party at Methuen to launch the *Brand New Bok*. No famous names, instead representatives of the printers, blockmakers, binders, etc., who had been involved in actually making the book. During the party Gledhill had very good news about the NFFC,[1] who were only too keen to go ahead with Python, White, Goldstone. [He] had with him a sheet of Heads of Proposals, which towards the end of the party he was getting people to sign. I couldn't take much of it in at that time, but seeing other signatures, and presuming it was merely a contract for story development in order to get the £6,000 front money, I too, signed.

Monday, November 5th

Another Python meeting *chez* Cleese. When I arrived there at 1.00 John Gledhill was sitting on the arm of a sofa looking wide-eyed and uncomfortable. Also there were Mark, John Cleese, Eric and Graham. No one seemed to be talking to each other. It was like a morgue. Then Terry J and Gilliam arrived, and we walked up to Tethers for lunch and a chat.

Once in Tethers, Terry J asked Mark to outline his criticisms of the contract which John Gledhill had asked us to sign at the book launching party last Thursday night. As Mark ran through the clauses, it was increasingly clear that we were being asked to sign away our copyright on the film – which is tantamount to signing away every bargaining counter Python ever had. Mark will draft a new agreement, with his solicitor, and we will present it to Goldstone later in the week.

1. National Film Finance Corporation, government-sponsored with money to invest in British films.

Tuesday, November 13th

Met with Jimmy Gilbert at BBC in the morning.[1] Jimmy, very genial, welcoming – very much the feeling of a nostalgic reunion, for all of us, except Gilliam, had helped to keep Jimmy in material for two series of *Frost Reports*.

I'm not sure if he really grasped what we wanted – which was, in effect, a new series of Python, without John, and different in style from the others by being unified, organic half-hours, and not just bric-a-brac, loosely slung together.

Monday, November 19th

Down to Terry's for another meeting on the film. Some good stuff from Eric – and some of the pieces I'd written at S'wold went down well, which was encouraging. At lunchtime Terry had a shouting match with John which blew up from nowhere. It was all about T feeling oppressed by John's rather dismissive handling of any suggestion of Terry's. In fact, John is trying to be fairly accommodating, but he does tend to dominate the group more than he used to.

Tuesday, November 27th

Worked at Terry's in the morning. We both seemed unable to summon up excitement or concentration about the film. The most I could manage was a sketch about Galahad having smelly breath.[2]

We took in one hour of Pasolini's *Canterbury Tales*, which Terry G had recommended. Superb recreation of medieval England – the kind of style and quality of shooting that we must get in our film, to stop it being just another *Carry On King Arthur*.

Wednesday, November 28th

Met at TG's later. He has been reading various fine-looking books on medieval warfare, and found that much of the absurd stuff that has already been written for the *Holy Grail* film has healthy precedents

---

1. He'd just been promoted to Head of Comedy.
2. Prompted by my reading out a sketch about a knight using coconuts instead of a horse, we agreed around this time to investigate the King Arthur story as a basis for the new film.

(e.g. taunting one's opponents and, as a last resort, firing dead animals at them during a siege – both quoted as medieval tactics by Montgomery). Then over to John's for a script meeting.

Mark F was there. The film deal is still not finalised. Apparently our Fairy Godmother, Michael White, is being quite businesslike with us – his cohort, John Goldstone, wants 12½% and a fee for a job whose function we cannot quite pin down, and Michael White wants his name prominently on the credits, plus various controls and final word on appointment of crew, production staff, editing, etc. So Mark has not signed yet. At the same time, Tony Stratton-Smith has come up with an offer of £45,000 from Pink Floyd, so there are alternative sources giving us a stronger hand against White.

Friday, December 28th

The film script was completed on Friday 14th – but still without enough group work on the links and plot scenes. But some very funny writing from all sources, Graham and John in particular were back on form.

1973 is the year which saw the break-up of the Python group. I was unable to accept that it was happening – indeed there were possibly more combined projects in 1973 than in 1972. The *Brand New Bok*, the 'First Farewell Tour' from April to June, the *Matching Tie and Handkerchief* LP, the film script. But all these projects were, to a certain extent, Python cashing in on a comfortably receptive market, rather than breaking new ground. The only project of '73 requiring new creative effort was the film – and although much good new material came up, there was nothing like the unified enthusiasm of the first two series.

Friday, January 4th, 1974

Met with Graham and John Gledhill at lunchtime. Graham is going to assemble a trial script for Jimmy Gilbert at the BBC to satisfy their need to see what Python may be like without John. A humiliating experience to start the year with. John Gledhill has at last some money from the Canadian tour – £350 each, but JG has managed to get us assurances of £1,500 each for a week at the Theatre Royal, Drury Lane in February.

Tuesday, January 15th, Southwold

Python meeting at T Gilliam's. We decide to do two weeks at Drury Lane, though I have a feeling in my bones that we would have done better to concentrate on one smash-hit week and leave people wanting more.

There was some fairly bitter debate over timing of the film and rewriting. In the end, we got down to some fast and efficient business, dates were agreed and there was a very useful hour's discussion of the film. An idea I had for the gradual and increasing involvement of the present day in this otherwise historical film was adopted as a new and better way of ending it, so I felt that I had done a bit of useful work over the last hectic month.

We decide to call our Drury Lane show 'Monty Python's First Farewell Tour (repeat)' and overprint it with the words 'NOT CANCELLED'.

Thursday, January 17th

At lunchtime, met Tony Smith, John Gledhill, Terry J, Terry G and André at Drury Lane to have a first look at the theatre in which we will be spending two weeks at the end of February. The approach to the auditorium, the passageways, and halls, are furnished and decorated in the grand classical style. It somehow feels as likely and as suitable a venue for Python as a power station. The size of the auditorium would a year ago have made me laugh and run out straight away to return Tony's contract, but having rehearsed in the Rainbow, and played the Wilfred Pelletier Theatre in Montreal, both of which hold over 3,000 seats, the wide-open spaces of the Theatre Royal (2,200 seats) no longer hold quite the same terror.

Friday, January 18th

GC and I, at GC's suggestion, went to the BBC to talk to Jimmy, who is vacillating still over a BBC series.

It seemed as though some decision had been made in the Beeb to treat us nicely again, and Graham and I completed a tidy half-day's work on behalf of Python by collecting a list of seven studio recording dates from Jimmy G, which, being in November, would fit in well with our year's schedule.

Suddenly it seems that 1974 could be our busiest and most creative since '71.

JG told us that to date *The Brand New Monty Python Bok* has sold 161,000 copies, and the new record is selling faster than any of the previous ones.

Thursday, January 24th

A press party to launch our two-week 'season' at the end of February. Up the wide staircase to the Circle bar, with four huge Corinthian columns dwarfing a motley collection of about thirty press folk.

Sunday, March 3rd

We have now completed seven shows at Drury Lane – ending last week with a grand flourish of two shows on Friday and two shows on Saturday. Kean and other great British actors of the past would have turned in their graves if they could have seen the front row full of Gumby-knotted handkerchiefs on the opening night on Tuesday.

The reviews have been surprisingly extensive – it takes a second-hand collection of old TV material for critics to start taking Python really seriously. Harold Hobson was greatly impressed and called us true Popular Theatre – and Milton Shulman, perhaps our first critical friend on the TV series, was equally enthusiastic.

We're in the fortunate position of not having to rely on reviews to sell our seats. Despite the fact that Drury Lane holds 2,200 people, we are booked solid for two weeks, we have extended our run to three weeks, and at every performance there are apparently touts out the front selling tickets for £5–£10.

Monday, March 4th

Into our second week at Drury Lane, and a lot of business to do during the day.

Meet with the Henshaws[1] and Nancy L[ewis], and Ina [Lee Meibach].[2] Under discussion was Nancy's official future with Python. At a recent meeting we decided to put Nancy in charge of our new music publishing company, Kay-Gee-Bee Music Ltd, and also to give her control of records and recordings and all future contracts.

Ina waxed lyrical about the future of Python in the States – and rather frightened everyone by talking of a 15% fee for Nancy's work. We still see our roots as an English TV comedy show, and I think we are all wary of the American monster, where everything can be so BIG and success can be so ENORMOUS and so on and so on.

Friday, March 15th

An easier week, this third one. Tonight is our last show of the week, and we also had Tuesday off. We have at last completed the Python film script. Terry and I, as usual, did most of the rewriting. It took us a week and a half of very solid work – the film is now shorter and has more shape.

This morning we met at Terry Gilliam's at 10.30 to read through our rewrites. The BBC had a sound team there. They are anxious to do an *Omnibus* programme on Python. None of us is particularly keen to be subjected to the sort of documentary which we're always sending up, so we were all a bit lukewarm towards the slightly pushy producer who was present at our meeting. A concentrated three-hour session on the film. Little argument, except over the 'Anthrax' sequence, and at 2.00 we had agreed on a final script.

Friday, March 22nd

The week's audiences have been capacity, apart from Monday and Tuesday, and, rather than become jaded, the show has brightened up

---

1. Michael Henshaw had been my accountant since 1966. His wife Anne was helping sort out Python's affairs.
2. Nancy's lawyer in New York.

a bit, and we're enjoying it more than ever. John has added little embellishments to 'Silly Walks' in order to corpse me. Terry and Graham, as the two Pepperpots, have a continuing battle with each other centring around lipstick and names. Graham's lipstick tonight stretched round his mouth, up and over the top of his nose; Terry had a phone number written in lipstick across his chest. They also have fun with names – starting by calling each other comparatively simple medical names (Mrs Scrotum, Mrs Orgasm), they have now become wonderfully obscure – Mrs Vas Deferens – and tonight's masterpiece from Graham was Madame Émission Nocturnelle.

Saturday, April 6th

After lunch today Eric and Graham came round for what was to have been a Python (less John) meeting re: the new TV series.

We have to decide whether or not the VTR [Video Tape Recording] dates which Jimmy provided in February are still practical. Things look bleak. The dates were fixed at a time when we were only doing two weeks at Drury Lane instead of four, and we have enormously underestimated the amount of time which the two Terrys will have to spend on the film. They will neither of them be able to concentrate for any length of time on a new TV series until late August – which is when Ian wants all the scripts in. So either Graham, Eric and I write all the scripts, which I think is out of the question, or we make an awkward compromise and start to film one month later, or we put the whole thing off until the spring.

Sunday, April 7th

Rang Terry J. He was of the opinion that it would be impolitic to alienate the BBC by refusing at this stage to do a series it had taken so long to set up. As Terry's attitude was a rather key factor (for he will have to work incredibly hard if he is to contribute much to the series *and* edit the Python film) I was quite heartened. Certainly the most comfortable solution would be to do the series on the dates offered.

Monday, April 8th

Tony Stratton–Smith rang in the evening – he had been listening to the 'Python Live at Drury Lane' tapes and was enthusing as only Strat can. He wanted to release a live album in June, as the high point of a Python month – a big promotional push to boost sales of all our LPs. Tony reckons this Python month could shift another 80,000 or 90,000 of our records, which, as he says, would keep us off the breadline during the summer! A lucky coup is that *NME* (*New Musical Express*) want to issue 400,000 Python flimsies [floppy 7-inch LPs recorded on one side only] as a giveaway with their paper in late May.

Filming *Monty Python and the Holy Grail* (April–May 1974)

1974

Monday, April 29th, Ballachulish, Scotland

We have been in Scotland a little over twenty-four hours. Scotland has been very welcoming, and I feel relaxed and comfortable and invigorated here after a busy two weeks.

During that time we rehearsed the film (*Monty Python and the Holy Grail*), and inevitably rewrote some of the scenes as we did so. But it came to life during rehearsal – we began to laugh at each other's performances again, and from being rather an albatross of worry round our necks (finance, script, etc., etc.), the film became enjoyable and fun.

Tuesday, April 30th, Ballachulish

First day of filming. Woken at 6.45. Sunshine streaming through the curtains. Into chainmail and red-cross tabard. A difficult day today – the Bridge of Death scene where Eric and I die and Lancelot is arrested by the police. Dangerous too – from what I hear.

Such is the economy on this film that not only do the actors have a minibus rather than cars to go to the location, but they also have to drive it.

John (Lancelot) and I (Galahad) driving up through Glencoe in a Budget Rent-a-Van in full chainmail.

Scrambled up to the Gorge of Eternal Peril – this took about fifteen minutes of hard climbing.

Camera broke midway through first shot.

The day is hastily rearranged and, from having been busy, but organised, it was now busy and disorganised. The sun disappeared. John Horton's smoke bombs and flames worked superbly. Graham as King Arthur got vertigo and couldn't go across the bridge.

Terry J comes up to me in the afternoon and says he's a bit worried about Terry G's priorities in choice of shots'[1] – we run two and a quarter hours overtime, until nearly 8.00. Everyone in the young unit seems happy enough.

Enjoyed the sight of Hamish MacInnes, Head of Mountain Rescue in Glencoe, flinging rubber corpses of knights into the gorge. More terrifying ledges to climb round on tomorrow.

Wednesday, May 1st, Ballachulish

At about 3.30 the call comes. Sir Robin and Sir Lancelot drive their Budget Rent-a-Van up to Glencoe, complete with a message from the producer to say we must stop by 6.00. At about 6.00 we are hanging onto the ledge above the gorge waiting for a long shot of the Bridge of Death. Terry J directs Terry G to get some more dirt on his legs (as the Soothsayer).

Then suddenly John Horton's effects go off, a few flares, firecrackers, smoke bombs, then, surprising everybody, huge mortar blasts which send scorching barrels of fire high into the air – the grass and trees are burning. No one (except John H) knows where the next blast will come from. Gerry Harrison [First Assistant Director] shouts, TJ shouts. John's stand-in races across the bridge with suicidal courage, only to be told to get back again as the camera can't see anything through the smoke.

Rather sad notices around Ballachulish today asking for volunteers to join an army for a scene tomorrow. They're only getting £2, and I think even the Scots will baulk at that.

Thursday, May 2nd, Ballachulish

Graham is getting shit poured all over him. He's taking a great deal of punishment in these first few days of filming.

---

1. *Monty Python and the Holy Grail* was directed by both Terry Jones and Terry Gilliam.

Wonderful chaos round about 4.00. Out on the island the motor-boat which drove the wondrous ship in which Arthur and Belvedere reached the Castle Aaargh! broke down and Terry J was left drifting across Loch Leven with the radio communication set. Terry G, in great Errol Flynn style, leapt into another dinghy, pushed it out with a flourish, but failed to make the engine work and was left also drifting about twenty yards out to sea. The whole scene, enacted in front of a motley army of extras, was great entertainment value – and cheered everyone up enormously.

Finally, frenetically, the army shot was completed, and, going into heavy overtime yet again, the day finished about 6.20. Or rather didn't finish, because we then had to drive to Killin on Loch Tay, our next location.

Friday, May 3rd, Killin

We are filming in a cave three or four miles beyond Ardeonaig, and the road winds rather prettily along the side of Loch Tay. From where we are filming – a rather tough ten-minute climb from the road – you can look down the length of Loch Tay and across the other side to the mountains, tipped by Ben Lawers (nearly 4,000 feet). A spectacular location, but soon filled with the flotsam and jet-sam of filming – boxes of equipment, tea urns, Land Rovers churning up and down the hill with lights, and wood for the construction team.

A slow day's filming, it seems. Rather a lot of worried faces when we run into overtime again. Hazel [Pethig, Costume Designer] especially has hardly had a moment to organise herself and her costumes, and looks completely shattered.

Julian [Doyle, Production Manager] took me aside after filming today as we walked down the hillside and said he was worried that the way things were being shot this week was putting a big strain on the budget (almost the entire £1,000 allowed for overtime was spent in this first week) and there would have to be some compromises by the Terrys somewhere along the line.

So we had a meeting at the Killin Hotel tonight in among the costumes, and the production/direction points of view were put forward. I think Terry G accepted that they would have to simplify the shooting script and perhaps compromise on some of the locations. It was also decided not to move to Doune until Monday.[1]

Saturday, May 4th, Killin

A good day's filming at last. Even John and Eric aren't grumbling, even though we go into overtime again. John Horton's rabbit effects are superb. A really vicious white rabbit, which bites Sir Bors' head off.

More good rushes in the evening. The boat takes them across to the Castle Aaargh! Looks really magical. It will give the film just the right kind of atmosphere and build-up to make the non-ending work. Terry Bedford's[2] effects, especially his fondness for diffusing the light, work superbly.

Monday, May 6th, Killin

Eric and I dressed as monks (gear that really rather suits us) toiling up to the cave at 8.30. Very clear sky, and the sun is already hot. Quite a long piece for me today as the monk who reads the instructions about the Holy Hand Grenade. As the sun is so bright, all the camera angles have to be changed, and the actors, so much fodder in the process of film-making, find themselves standing on a steep slope, precariously perched barefoot on rather slippery mud. All the knights are in the stream down below. Terry J gives me a good piece of direction which makes my perf. more silly and lively. But it is a hard morning's work for everybody. For the first time we see the pages – they are weighed down with very heavy packs and their first movements have to be uphill over rather difficult terrain. Everyone very near the end of their tether – Graham shaking and quivering with suppressed neurotic rage – when lunch break is called at 2.30.

And so to Doune at 10.00. This is to be our home for the next two weeks.

---

1. The Scottish National Trust had vetoed most of our castle locations, deeming the script 'not consistent with the dignity of the fabric of the buildings'. Doune was a privately owned castle.
2. Director of Photography.

Tuesday, May 7th

Today we shoot the Camelot musical sequence. A long and busy day for fifty seconds' worth of film. Dancers dressed as knights wrecking Camelot. In the middle of the day Mark has arranged a press call, but as the two Terrys are busy directing, the brunt falls on Eric, Neil [Innes], John and myself. The usual questions: who is Monty Python? How did you all get together? Obvious questions maybe, but they drive us potty. Lots of photos – can you all put your heads round the shields?, etc. Eric and Neil try to escape, Colditz style, by walking out of the gate when Mark isn't looking, talking terribly urgently to each other – they made it back to the hotel before being recaptured.

Wednesday, May 8th

The first of two and a half days on the Castle Anthrax scene.

Spent the morning being drenched by the Perth and Kinross Fire Brigade. Next time I shall think twice about writing a scene in a raging storm. I start behind camera, and before 'Action!' I am solemnly wetted down by Tommy Raeburn of Props, with a little greenhouse watering can. I then rush up through rain provided by a fireman from behind a bush, to a castle made of cardboard.

Thursday, May 8th

This was the second day on Castle Anthrax. Doune Castle's severe granite halls are now filled with about twenty girls in diaphanous white gowns, shivering against the cold. The bathing scene takes two hours to set up – the girls giggle a lot, and generally it's about as sexy as a British Legion parade.

We shoot on late – until 7.30 or so – utterly shattered – but Carol C stood up to it remarkably well and was v. funny. Like Neil, she is an honorary Python, and has very little trouble in clicking into our way of doing things.

Friday, May 10th

9.30: In Anthrax Castle again, with Tommy poised with watering can.

'Michael, can you fall about six inches to your left?' after I have crashed onto the stone floor for three rehearsals already.

11.00: Still waiting for the shot. Terry J, who tends to become very Ian MacN-like sometimes – 'Come on, now *quick*, we must get this shot in before 11.25, we really *must!*' Terry G is working away more quietly with the camera crew, checking the shot, putting a candle in foreground here and there. Gerry Harrison, for all his sometimes alienating head-prefect manner, is always very accessible and can get a cup of coffee for shivering actors.

Out in the main courtyard of the castle, a BBC crew from *Film Night* are interviewing Graham C.

We finish Anthrax with a last v. good take, especially from Carol, and that sequence is now finished, and we go out to the front of the castle.

The BBC doggedly film the filming. Cardboard battlements have to be added on to the castle before John does his taunting. 'John! Don't lean too heavily on the battlements, you can see them bending.'

At about 4.30 there are a few distant claps of thunder, the sky turns a fine deep grey – which Terry Bedford is very pleased about – and we get one shot in with this background before an enormous cloudburst empties the field in front of the castle.

Saturday, May 11th

John is doing the Taunter on some artificial battlements at the back of the castle. He's getting very irritated by TG's direction of his acting. TG tends to communicate by instinct, gesture and feeling, whereas John prefers precise verbal instructions. So TJ has to take over and soothe John down.

Then the shot where live ducks and chickens, as well as dead rabbits, badgers, etc., are flying over the battlements. Small boys are recruited to help catch the chickens as they're flung over.

A rather jolly day, with much corpsing from John, Eric and myself when Brian McNulty, Third Assistant Director, in rich Glaswegian, reads in John's Taunter's lines for us to react to. How can you react without laughing to a broad Glaswegian saying 'Of course I'm French, why do you think I'm using this outrageous accent?'

Monday, May 13th

The day of the Mud-Eater. Clad in rags, crawling through filthy mud repeatedly and doggedly, in a scene which makes the flagellation scene from *Seventh Seal* look like *Breakfast at Tiffany's*. Extras all supposed to have plague – boils and pustules everywhere. People really do look wretched and, after two hours wallowing in the mud, because the plague village is such a convincing set, reality becomes fantasy and fantasy becomes reality. The camera crew, the scrubbed and well-dressed line of faces looking at us and occasionally turning a big black machine towards us, seems quite unreal, a horrible dream.

At the end of the day I have to eat mud. John Horton prepares a mixture of currants, chocolate instant whip, pieces of fruit cake and cocoa, and pours it out onto a patch of soil from which it is indistinguishable.

Monday, May 20th

Spent a day in the hills above Callander doing a great deal of silly riding.

Strange surreal moment: a wooden cut-out of Camelot, which stood on the top of the hill, and looked utterly three-dimensional and realistic, suddenly blew away.

Friday, May 24th

Filming is an appalling process for reducing an actor to the role of machine. In the Knights of Ni, for instance, I was to do close-ups first. Directly in front of me are a group of anoraked people squatting down, far more preoccupied with their equipment than with me. Someone reads the lines off in a flat voice, which gives you little encouragement. An eyeline keeps you looking at no one at all. Two huge white polystyrene reflectors enclose me on either side – it feels like acting in a sandwich. Then you are about to start and the sound isn't right – and then the sun comes out and that isn't right, as the camera focus has to be adjusted – and during this so much of one's spontaneity and relaxation just drain away.

Tuesday, May 28th

Today we are to shoot Robin and the Singers' encounter with the Three-Headed Knight. But Graham, who is one of the three heads – the other two being myself and Terry – is not back from London. It's a complicated piece of learning, which needs all of us to rehearse it properly, and in the last week or so Graham has lost all his early confidence over lines.

Graham, Terry and I huddle into the cab of the camera van to learn the words. (One thing we MUST have on future filming is a caravan or, even better, a Dormobile, which is purely for the actors to use. When there is nowhere to sit, nowhere to relax while they spend one and a half hours setting up the shoot, one can get very ratty.)

Finally we are strapped into our Three-Headed Knight costume at about 5.00. All my apprehensions about it were unfulfilled. Graham, with just a little prompting, was fluent and funny, and Terry J was the one who seemed to be physically suffering in the uncomfortable costume.

Wednesday, May 29th

John, dressed as a magician, spent much of the morning on the narrow top of an extremely impressive pinnacle of slate, across the quarry from us.

Twice the cameras turned. Twice John, towering above the green and pleasant vistas of the Trossachs, gave the signal to summon forth mighty explosions. Twice the explosions failed, and John was left on this striking, but lonely, pinnacle. He kept in good form, reciting his old cabaret monologues across the quarry, but it was a hard start to the day for him – and he was cold and subdued by the time he came back.

Once again it was a day where visual effects took the major amount of time, leaving John's quite long passages of dialogue to the later part of the afternoon. John's performance was good, but he had passed the point when it might have become inspired. But then you never know on film.

Thursday, May 30th

God appeared to us in the morning – with the help of John Horton's fireworks.

Finally called to do the opening sequence of the film at the end of the day. Usual difficulty with 'swirling mist', as it was a totally unmisty day. But beautiful views all around from the castle battlements – rolling green hills stretching into the distance, tranquillity, peace.

Tomorrow is the last day of filming. Already an end–of–term atmosphere.

Friday, May 31st

Today is cloudy, and it's been raining quite hard in the night. The long and wordy Constitutional Peasants scene. Arrive at a bleak location in the hills above Callander. Mud is being prepared.

Terry Bedford is angry because Mark has been trying to economise by buying old film stock. Some of the film which has arrived today is six years old. Terry will not use it – in fact he threw a can into a nearby moorland stream – so we have 1,000 feet on which to do this entire scene. Very little chance of retakes. Somehow it takes a supreme effort to get the words and the character together. We do the scene in one long master shot and, thank God, we get through without a hitch. Ideally would have liked another take – just to see if any part of the performance would be better, but there is not enough time or enough film. The day gets greyer as it progresses, blending perfectly with our peasants' costumes and mirroring the generally downtrodden air.

That night, back at the hotel, I had a drink with Tommy Raeburn and the other chippies and drivers – hard men of films, who nevertheless reckoned the chances of the film's success to be very good. Roy Smith, the Art Director, said he wished he had money in it.

Editing *Monty Python
and the Holy Grail*;
launch of the fifth record album:
Monty Python Live at Drury Lane;
work on fourth television series
(June–November 1974)

1974

Wednesday, June 5th

Today I talked to Gail at Charisma. She says that 70,000 copies of the *Live at Drury Lane* album are being pressed, though not at EMI – for the lady pressers there, whose unofficial censorship we have come up against before, would not consider dealing with a record containing, as Gail put it, 'three fucks and a dagger up the clitoris'.

At 4.30 we met at Henshaw's. We talked about various points, including a fund, from our film proceeds, to give most of the main members of the crew a share in the profits. This was agreed, in principle, to be a good thing.

Monday, June 24th

This morning we saw a rough cut of the film. In its raw state, without dubbing, sound fx, music and any editing guidance by the two Terrys, it tends to be rather heavy in certain scenes – but there are set pieces like the Plague Village, the fight with the Rabbit and the Holy Hand Grenade which work very well, even at this stage, and the recently filmed Black Knight fight wasn't in, which I hear is also a great set piece.

The only scene which I felt was seriously deficient at this stage is the appearance of the Three-Headed Knight. It just doesn't look imposing enough, and very similar in set-up to the Knights of Ni.

Wednesday, July 3rd

Started work at 9.15 (on new Python TV series) and by lunchtime had 'The Golden Age of Ballooning' typed and organised into a twenty-nine-page script, which could do as a half-hour on its own. Feel rather pleased, as it is almost entirely my own work.

Up to the Angel at Highgate to meet Graham. I looked through the work on the 'Michael Ellis' script which G and I had worked on together. Some good ideas there – and it made me laugh. Also made me aware of the usefulness of co-writing, after my euphoria of the morning! There are just jokes and ideas in the 'Michael Ellis' script which I would never have made as funny if I had been writing on my own.

Thursday, July 11th

Writing with Graham. Graham is a very good person to write dialogue with, and has very good silly ideas, but there is a rather uncomfortably undisciplined feeling to the day's work. We manage about two hours in the morning, before he starts getting really fidgety, then two more hours in the afternoon. Whereas Terry and myself, when we have a full day's writing, put in about six and a half solid hours.

Sunday, July 14th

It's a busy week ahead, as Eric is back from France today for two weeks, and, by some sort of Herculean effort, we should have most of the six new TV shows mapped out by the time he goes back.

Monday, July 15th

The 'Ballooning' story, Mr Neutron and, read last, but appreciated most, the Michael Ellis 'Harrods Ant Counter', which I'd put together with GC, and typed up rather uncertainly on Friday, very well received, which was most encouraging.

Wednesday, July 24th

At 6.30 a Python business meeting at Henshaws'.

What was the meeting about? Oh, I think, what should we do with the Python fortunes when they really start coming in? Is it? I suppose so. After all, *Python Live at Drury Lane* does sound to be the bestseller of all our albums – No. 19 next week, according to Gail at Charisma.

Thursday, August 1st

Up to Graham's for our script meeting with Ian. Ian was drinking Scotch with dedicated frequency, inveighing against Terry Gilliam for wanting assistants for his animation, against Jill Foster (his, and our, agent) for some unspecified, but clearly deeply felt reason, us for trying to get shows in that were too long, and so on and so on.

I began to feel what was the point? Here was a series that only Graham was really keen to do, and yet only Terry and I were writing. Here was a series which we had, for better or worse, fought for from the BBC and, with not a few misgivings, we had asked for Ian only to direct it, and yet Ian comes back at us with a totally unrealistic 'this is my show, you do what I say' attitude.

Monday, August 12th

Stop Press: writing my diary at 11.15 when the phone rings. It's Nancy from New York, almost speechless with good news. As from October, the entire Python first series is being screened on American TV by PBS.[1]

Sunday, September 8th, Exeter

From today we start filming on the fourth Python series.

---

1. The Public Broadcasting Service (Channel 13). The only non-commercial channel on US television. It is supported by public subscription.

Friday, September 27th

Filming aboard HMS *Belfast* moored by the Tower of London. I was to go along there at lunchtime, meet them and prepare for quite a long sketch to be filmed on Westminster Bridge in the afternoon.

The morning's shot had been completed, but with much laughter amongst the crew of *Belfast* – for Graham was dressed as a captain in full drag.

The advantages of being dressed as a policeman are that I was able to stop four lanes of traffic on Westminster Bridge at rush hour, walk across the road, hit Terry, dressed as a lady, grab his armchair and walk back across the road with the cars still respectfully at a standstill!

One old lady approached me, stared hard at my false moustache and said, 'What are you? Real or a fake?'

'Have a guess,' I said.

She surveyed my loose moustache and pinned-up hair for a moment: 'You're real.'

Tuesday, October 1st

In the evening we had an investors' preview of *Monty Python and the Holy Grail* at the Hanover Grand.

Tony Stratton-Smith was there, and Ali and Brian Gibbons – the financial wizards behind Charisma.

Mark had to make an announcement before the film explaining that it was not yet finally cut. But the result was even more disastrous than I'd thought. It was one of those evenings when Python flopped.

Undoubtedly the poor quality of the print hadn't helped. A couple of times there were booms in shot which killed the scenes after them. The soundtrack had been so realistically and thoroughly dubbed by Terry G and John Hackney that the slightly gory sequences had a sickening impact which didn't help loosen people up.

I didn't, I must admit, immediately look to technical faults to explain away my acute discomfort through most of the showing. I just felt, looking at it, that there were not enough jokes there. The film was 20% too strong on authenticity and 20% too weak on jokes.

Terry J clearly felt that what was wrong was there was too much animation and too noisy a soundtrack. Both faults of TG. Poor TG. He had to put up with stick from Mark and Michael White later in the evening, and has been working eighteen hours a day on the film.

Wednesday, October 2nd

Spent a most uncomfortable day in a studio jungle at Ealing, trying to portray the almost unparody-able David Attenborough. We got the make-up on, hair pinned up, bladder stuck on and wig over that. Then suddenly I made a face that caught Attenborough and made the whole ensemble work.

The discomfort of the make-up was nothing, compared to the special effect required to make Attenborough sweat profusely – this consisted of pipes thrust up my trouser legs and under my armpits and connected to the water supply for the studio. When the shot was eventually ready, it was impossible to do a fully practical rehearsal, so I was halfway into a take of a long speech when I felt ice-cold water pouring from my armpits.

From filming, I drove straight to Regent's Park and a Python film meeting. Michael White was the surprise guest – he had come along, he said, to tell us not to be too disheartened about the film. It was, in his opinion, far too bloodthirsty, far too unpleasant in its atmosphere; almost every scene, he complained, showed death, disease, dirt or destruction. It was not easy to take the whole White approach as The Word, but several aspects of it rang true.

TG stayed quiet and didn't fight. Graham bristled at every criticism of the violence – he regards it as important, honest, etc., etc. Terry J, like a cat with his hackles up whenever Mark's around, prowled the room, arguing fiercely that it should never have been shown in its unfinished state.

Thursday, October 3rd

Drove Graham down to Motspur Park, where we were filming a cricket match.

Ian has reverted to the spirits. In the afternoon he could hardly stand up, and at one point he actually fell backwards over the camera tripod.

Apart from this afternoon, Ian has been a changed man – confident, cooperative and always in control, both of us and the crew.

Saturday, October 5th

At 10.00 down to the Henshaws' for a meeting about the film with Eric, Terry G, Gra, Mark and John Hackney, the editor.

The meeting, which Terry J had wanted to make very brief, lasted solidly from 10.00 until 5.00. Everybody had their say about every part of the film. Eric and Mark won a point over the Three-Headed Knight, which is now back in for us to look at. The animation has been cut down (the first time I can remember in all Python history when we have actually chopped any of TG's stuff). Some of Neil's music was thought to be not right, so we are putting on a lot of stock music. We have lost more of the 'Ni' sequence. There was nearly deadlock over reshooting the very important opening joke with the coconuts. Mark clams up on any mention of reshooting, and TJ rises accordingly.

Monday, November 4th

As soon as we got to rehearsal today and started to read through the 'Mr Neutron' script, an almost tangible blanket of gloom fell on everyone. The script was bitty, and rather difficult to read, admittedly – it's a show where we only need ten minutes' studio – but this alone couldn't account for the unprecedentedly dolorous mood around the table.

Because Eric was in France for all but two weeks of the entire writing and planning stage of the series, there is very little of his contribution in the series. In a welter of bitterly delivered contradictions, he criticised us for not accepting his half-hour, and at the same time bemoaned the fact that we wrote half-hours at all. He didn't like writing stories, he liked writing revue.

At lunchtime came a fresh jolt from the BBC. In Graham's speech as the Icelandic Honey Week rep – very funny and all recorded – they wanted the lines 'Cold enough to freeze your balls off, freeze the little buggers solid in mid-air' cut from the tape, as well as one 'piss off' (we could keep the other). Jimmy had apparently said very strongly to Ian that 'if and when Python Productions made their own series they could say what they like', but for now they must accept what the BBC say. Censorship, in fact. Yes, says Jimmy, it is 'censorship'. We had already burned off most of our frustrated anger at the BBC's decision to omit the word 'condom' from that show. I mean, if condom is considered a bannable word on British TV in 1974, what hope is there.

One of Jimmy's reasons for this fresh bout of anti-sexual censorship is that we are going out at 8.30 on BBC1 when the shows are repeated. Do we let the BBC change Python into a soft, inoffensive half-hour of pap, or do we fight to keep its teeth, its offensiveness, its naughtiness?

Tuesday November 5th

Robert [Hewison, who wrote and performed with Michael at Oxford] thinks we ought to stop Python whilst we're still at the top. I think thirty-one is a little early to quit – but a few more mornings like yesterday could change my mind.

Wednesday, November 6th

Rehearsals a lot more convivial today, but Graham is feeling very low, as in Monday's editing Terry and Ian decided that, in view of the censorship cuts demanded by the BBC, the entire Icelandic Honey Week speech from Show 2 would have to be taken out. The loss of three sentences at the BBC's behest has therefore effectively castrated a funny, absurd, harmless and well-performed little piece.

Anne Henshaw[1] came to the rehearsals to give us some money from the book (which seems set for some good sales again this Christmas – the *Papperbok* is No. 3 in the best-selling lists), and she also showed us a letter from the financial frontman at Charisma, which tried to argue that we were not owed £11,000, but nearer £6,000. This is clearly not true, so the situation there is deteriorating rapidly.

---

1. Anne had taken over as our manager from John Gledhill.

Friday, November 8th

Nancy rang from New York to say she was ecstatic about the critical success of the TV show in New York. Boston and Philadelphia have bought the show.

Saturday, November 9th

Our fifth recording. Not a great deal of pressure this week as nineteen minutes of the show are on film. So it all goes smoothly and unremarkably.

At the end of the dress runthrough, Jimmy Gilbert appeared, a little awkward perhaps, but clearly on placatory mission. Great show last week, he said, and apparently the viewing figures – at 5.8 million for Show 1 of the fourth series – were the best on BBC2 apart from *Call My Bluff*!!

Wednesday, November 13th

After rehearsal today Anne Henshaw came to tell us that Charisma are, in fact, broke. How serious it is we don't know – but at least they admit that we are owed £13,000, and presumably this money increases every time someone buys one of our records.

Tuesday, November 19th

Python flourishes. Our third show finally seems to have brought people back to the fold. Both the *Sunday Times* and the *Observer* noted this weekend that the show was back on 'cracking form' (the *Sunday Times*). We recorded our last show on Saturday – to a very receptive audience, which was most encouraging. The BBC, or rather J Gilbert on the phone to G Chapman, have confirmed that they want us to do seven more shows in the spring, and Eric was heard on Saturday night to agree to doing them – provided there are plenty of sketches and not so many storylines.

A further television series considered;
the television series launched in the US;
Monty Python and the Holy Grail
opens in the UK;
the *Holy Grail* record album
(November 1974–April 1975)

1974-1975

Friday, November 29th

5.30: Arrive at 22 Park Square East (Michael and Anne Henshaw's home) for a Python meeting. Nothing of great interest until we start, in the absence of JC, to discuss 'Next Year'.

Eric: 'Does anyone feel like me that the TV series has been a failure?'

TG and I are both keen to do another seven. I am decided in my own mind that the last six have been good enough, and well-received enough, to try and complete a further seven – as a group, using TG and Eric more fully and TJ and MP less.

Then, after half an hour or so, Eric is suddenly agreeing, not only to the series, but to a rescheduling of dates taking us up to July. He doesn't look all that happy, but he seems to have agreed. So Python carries on. Then we elect a new Chairman by playing stone and scissors. I win, so Terry G has to be the new Chairman.

Saturday, November 30th

Eric goes through his reasons for dissatisfaction. He feels Python no longer works as a group. The formula is dull, we no longer surprise and shock, we are predictable. But he clearly misses John a great deal. None of us are as good as John or ever will be, he says.

Sunday, December 1st

Grey, but dry day. Two long phone calls re: Python in the morning to TG and TJ. I have an instinctive warmth towards TJ – and yet

TG is the only person whom I can now talk to fully and objectively about Monty P.

Thursday, January 9th, 1975

Another sign of the times. The Beatles' company, Beatles Ltd, officially and finally ceased to exist today. The group haven't played together since 1969. We began when they finished.

Friday, January 10th

By one of those strange coincidences, today was the day that Python and the Beatles came together. In the last two months we've heard that George H has been using 'Lumberjack Song' from the first BBC LP as a curtain-raiser to his US stage tour.

Terry J, Graham and myself on behalf of Python and Neil Aspinall and Derek Taylor[1] on behalf of the Beatles, found ourselves at lunchtime today in a hastily converted office at the Apple Corp's temporary headquarters in smart St James's, to watch the *Magical Mystery Tour* – the Beatles' TV film made in 1967. When it was suggested at a meeting late last year that we should try and put out the *Magical Mystery Tour* as a supporting film to the *Holy Grail*, there was unanimous agreement among the Python group.

Unfortunately it was not an unjustly underrated work. However, it *is* extraordinary still, and many sequences are very successful. It's also quite long – nearly an hour. It will have great curiosity value and should be complementary to the Python film, because much of it looks like familiar Python territory.

I was given George Harrison's number by Aspinall, who said he thought George would appreciate a call. Later in the evening I phoned George Hargreaves (as Derek Taylor and Aspinall referred to him). George and I chatted for about twenty minutes or so. He adores the shows so much – 'The only sane thing on television.'

---

1. Neil was the closest to a manager the Beatles had at the time; Derek was the press officer.

Monday, January 27th

Terry Gilliam rang about 9.30 and set off a whole chain of calls which resulted in a total replanning of the year ahead.

TG had seen Ian MacNaughton at Sölden. On the slopes, Ian told TG that he was highly dissatisfied with the way the BBC were treating him. He has a job in Israel, which would prevent him from working on the Python TV show until May (i.e. until after our filming). So it appears that, if we want Ian to direct our shows, and I think everybody does, we cannot start filming until May. This would mean studio dates running into August, which I know will be unacceptable so, as TG said, the alternative is to put it all off.

The more I thought about it, the more attractive postponement of the recordings became. TJ was keen and, when I rang Eric, he was not only keen, but as positive about Python as I've heard him in a long while.

Tuesday, February 4th

Good news from New York – Python is top of the PBS Channel 13 ratings there, beating even *Upstairs, Downstairs*, which has just won an Emmy and all. Sales to other stations increase.

Thursday, February 6th

We have written a synopsis of the *Holy Grail* for the EMI publicity people. Eric wrote it some time ago, and it is extremely funny and totally unrelated to anything that happens in the film.

Wednesday, February 19th

Today was a sunny, brilliantly sunny, neo-spring morning, for the first gathering of all the Pythons for six months or so. There is a good feeling to the group, and, when we start to talk about publicity ideas, the chemistry works and ideas bubble out in a stream.

When we suggest a 'Dummy Premiere in the presence of Her Royal Highness the Dummy Princess Margaret'[1] – with a car laid on

---

1. The life-size Dummy Princess Margaret had been created for the Python TV series and, rather than leave her in the props store, we used her to add a bit of class to the Drury Lane stage show, in which she occupied a box throughout the run.

to transport this now famous Python dummy lady to the theatre, and all of us lined up shaking hands – Mark says that EMI just wouldn't wear it. Terry J said, 'Mark, if you don't feel that you can fight EMI for the things we want, then someone else ought to be doing the job.'

Well, at the end of the meeting, Mark is still doing the job.

Thursday, February 20th

Another Python meeting. Good news at the beginning. Nancy rang through to say that a US record deal was signed today with Arista Records – we would get an immediate $10,000 advance on *Matching Tie* and *Live at Drury Lane*. So good work there from Nancy, who has also secured her pet consideration on a record contract – $50,000 set aside just for publicity.

It was on the subject of paying off Gledhill[1] that the meeting suddenly and abruptly took off. Eric became quite animated, attacking the Terrys and anyone around for being mean with Gledhill. From here Eric went on bitterly to criticise Python for becoming nothing more than a series of meetings, calling us 'capitalists' and ending up by saying, 'Why can't we get back to what we enjoyed doing?'

Terry J was on his feet – 'Well, if that's how Eric feels, we might as well give up,' and he nearly left there and then. GC and JC looked at each other in amazement. Only the entirely admirable Anne H managed to cool everything down by giving out cheques for £800 each from Charisma – an advance for the LP made last May!

A selection of letters are read out to the assembled gathering. From CBC Canada – 'We would like the Python group to contribute up to ten minutes of material for a special programme on European Unity. The group can decide – ' the reading was interrupted here by farting noises and thumbs-down signs. On to the next.

'Dear Sirs, I am writing on behalf of the Television Department of Aberdeen University…' An even louder barrage of farting.

'Dear Monty Python, we are a production company interested in making TV films with Python, George Harrison and Elton John…' Despite the fact that £36,000 is mentioned in the letter as a possible fee for this never-to-be-repeated offer, it is jeered raucously and I tear the letter up and scatter it over the Henshaws' sitting room.

---

1. John Gledhill had ceased to be our manager as from November 1974.

Saturday, February 22nd

I noticed Eric's car outside the house and felt quite pleased. It proved that his mood on Thursday was just a mood. Eric said he wanted to talk. We went upstairs to my workroom.

Eric told me, again, but finally, this time, that he couldn't go on with Python. He'd thought about it a lot over the last few weeks, the decision hadn't come lightly – but he felt that he had to get out or he would, as he put it, 'go mad'. He hadn't anything he was going to do – he just wanted to enjoy the experience of 'waking up in the morning, knowing I don't have to do anything'.

I must admit I had slight pinch-of-salt feelings. At my most cynical I felt here is someone who has his own novel, and another virtually commissioned, about to come out, and his own TV series too (*Rutland Weekend Television*), and he is understandably anxious to shed his old Python skin. He's moving on, like John did. Oh, he did say in passing that if John came back to do a TV series he would come back too.

Eric and I parted on good terms. This evening could be the end of lots of things.

Monday, February 24th

To the Henshaws' for what could be yet another momentous Python meeting.

I'm the first there – Anne H hurries up the stairs with some coffee and says ruefully, 'This is going to be quite a morning, isn't it?' Graham arrives next. He takes the news of Eric's latest decision stoically to say the least. The two Terrys are equally resigned.

The news from America daily lends an extra air of unreality to the situation for, by all accounts, Python is catching on in the States as *the* prestige programme to watch. Nancy rings to say San Francisco has now taken the series. Python is set to become the latest cult amongst the AB readership group, whilst back in little old, quaint, provincial London, it has finally run its course, and four of its creators are sitting around deciding who is going to do the cleaning-up before the place is finally locked up for the year – or maybe for ever.

The new book is off for the summer, the TV series is off for the autumn. Touring seems the only hope of getting us together again.

But I do not feel, at this stage, that we can ring Tony S-Smith and change our minds once again over the album of the film. Eric and John have intimated that they are available to do any voices, but the way I feel at the moment, it's a matter of pride to do it without them.

As if not enough had happened today, Mark rings to say that we haven't got the Casino [in Old Compton Street, now the Prince Edward Theatre] for our West End opening – we are back to the ABC Bloomsbury, the Scene at the Swiss Centre and the ABC Fulham Road (now four cinemas).

Tuesday, February 25th

At 10.00 Graham and Douglas Adams arrive at Julia Street and, over coffee, we work out select front-of-house photos for all the cinemas and work out silly captions – then down to Soho to meet Jack Hogarth, Head of EMI Distribution, to try and put our arguments against an ABC Bloomsbury opening. How can you speak on equal terms to a man with forty square feet of polished wood between him and you?

Terry J took the lead, I tried to back him up, and GC said nothing. Not that there is much you can say when Terry is in the form he was today. He was away with guns blazing, and it was a joy to watch. Did *he* know we could pack any cinema anywhere? Did *he* know people had marched in sub-zero temperatures in Toronto to get the series put back on CBC? And so on.

Thursday, February 27th

The film and the film publicity is gathering an almost inexorable impetus. The good news is that EMI have put us into the Casino after all, and the incredible news is that they are simultaneously opening us at the ABC Bloomsbury and ABC Fulham Road.

A half-hour call from John Goldstone. He has had a letter back from the censor. The film cannot be given an 'A' (over-fives, accompanied), unless we cut down two gory moments, and lose one 'shit', the words 'oral sex', the entire phrase 'We can make castanets of your testicles' and some of King Arthur's repeated 'Jesus Christs'.

I was prepared to trade the 'shit' for the 'oral sex', otherwise we'll settle for an 'AA' (over-fourteen). It's all too silly.

Friday, February 28th

Up to G Chapman's for record writing. We listen (TG, TJ, Graham, Douglas and myself) to the tapes of the film. And surprisingly involving it is too.

Tuesday, March 4th

Down to Soho for a meeting at 11.00 with Stephen Murphy, the film censor.

Murphy has a donnish air; he chain-smokes and has a mischievous face and a slightly uncoordinated physical presence. But he's genial and easy and a wonderful change from the executives of EMI. Of course the censor is not a government watchdog, but a man appointed by the industry to protect itself, so there wasn't a great deal of unseen pressure as there is at the BBC in these sort of discussions. Jolly Mr Murphy claims he has done a great deal for us and, if we want this 'A' certificate (in order to make more money!) we must go a little way with him. So could we lose 'oral sex', 'shit' or any of the 'Jesus Christs'? '"Oral sex" is a problem,' he said, very seriously.

Well, we came out and, over a coffee in Compton Street, decided that we would agree on changing a couple of Arthur's angry 'Jesus Christs'! TJ eventually came up with a replacement. Arthur should say 'Stephen Murphy'!

As the American bandwagon rolled on, there was an almost insatiable demand for Pythons to help publicise the TV series on PBS and the release of a new record album. The two Terrys, Graham and myself agreed to go over.

Sunday, March 9th, New York

Over to Channel 13, which is in a small, cramped, but friendly basement a couple of blocks from the UN and on the edge of the East River. In the studio is a small presentation area, in which sits Gene Shalit, a genial Harpo Marx sort of character. The programmes of Channel 13 (which include English imports like *Upstairs, Downstairs* and *The Ascent of Man*) are interspersed with jolly sales pitches from

Gene in which he asks the audience to phone up and pledge money – five, ten dollars, whatever – to keep this non-commercial station going.

Two Python shows have gone out on Channel 13 that evening, plus at least half an hour's screen time of ourselves. At the end of the evening, on air, we make a very committed statement about public subscription television and the freedom which it brings. Python, as far as we are concerned, could never have gone out in the States without public broadcasting.

Monday, March 10th, New York

Today is dominated by a party, to be held at Sardi's restaurant, to launch us as new stars on Clive Davis's Arista label. The first thing that impressed me about the Great Man of the American Recording Business was his office. He had the kind of exaggerated fifteen-foot desk which we write into sketches, and yet you could see he needed it. It was full of papers, letters ready for signing, telephones, intercoms, etc., etc.

He was clearly feeling his way with the Python group. He may be World Expert on Dylan, Sonny and Cher and Blood, Sweat & Tears, but one got the feeling he was not yet certain about why he liked Python or why others liked Python.

Clive said a few words, we joked a little and then the 'Thomas Hardy Novel-Writing' track was played. I had to pinch myself to believe it was all happening. Were we really in Sardi's, the renowned Broadway restaurant, with Clive Davis, the renowned record producer, surrounded by a crowd 'ooohing!' and 'aaahing' with uncertain delight as a not-brilliant sketch about Thomas Hardy writing a novel was played over a hastily rigged-up record-player system?

Thursday, March 13th, Philadelphia

The morning spent at the Philadelphia PBS TV studios. We recorded some direct, almost sincere, straight-to-camera promos, extolling the thinking man's channel.

Saturday, March 15th, Dallas

Drove down to the PBS station, to find ourselves facing a barrage of microphones and reporters, who sat amongst the scenery and props, barring our way to the studio. It could have been awful, but as it was so spontaneous it was exhilarating.

After the 'press conference' we are moved through into the studio. We are in chairs on a podium and are chatted to at regular intervals by Ron Devillier,[1] programme director of the station. A lovely man, comfortably built, soft-voiced, bearded, about thirty-five to forty, with a lack of pretension and a great deal of knowledge and intelligence.

During the course of the evening they played no less than three Python shows. It was an orgy of Python – a total immersion in total enthusiasm, that didn't end until after 12.00.

Tuesday, March 25th

Grand Python reunion at the recording studio![2] All of us, except Terry Gilliam, contributing. John C had written a piece about a Professor of Logic. We recorded it first time. I think John's psychiatrist should be sent a copy. It was a funny piece, largely, but loaded with rather passionless and violent sexual references, which sounded odd, for some reason.

We decided that our next film would be 'Monty Python and the Life of Christ' – with Graham as Christ, and featuring exciting new characters like Ron the Baptist. We also decided with remarkably little fuss that we would all get together to do a six-week stage show in the US next spring.

Thursday, April 3rd

Today our second film opens in London. An encouragingly good notice in the *Guardian* this morning. A very good Alexander Walker review in the *Evening Standard* ('The brightest British comedy in

---

1. Ron was the man who broke *Monty Python's Flying Circus* on US television. Python's success began not in New York, but in Dallas.
2. André Jacquemin's new premises in Wardour Street.

ages') and *Time Out*, who've also enjoyed it, help to cheer us all up, for these two are influential amongst our London audience.

The film was very well received. Afterwards, a party had been laid on in the stalls bar (this entirely due to Anne H and Terry G's initiative) for all the crew (who had not been invited to the later party at the Marquee.)

Sunday, April 6th

The popular press, *News of the World*, *Daily* and *Sunday Express*, *Daily Mail*, *The People*, *The Sun*, have given us rave reviews. The *News of the World* even said that the credits on their own were funnier than most comedy films. The *Observer* joined *Sounds* and the *New Musical Express* in panning us.

Friday, April 11th

Grail is No. 3 in London this week, and has grossed nearly £19,000. The film's success in the last couple of weeks has helped to prolong Python's life and greatly increase its prestige.

Monty Python and the Holy Grail
opens in New York;
plans for a live stage show in New York;
legal challenge to ABC Television
goes to court
(April–December 1975)

1975

With Monty Python and the Holy Grail *set to open in New York, we set off across the Atlantic for the second time in a month.*

Friday, April 25th, New York

To the ABC *A.M. America* studios. We (the Pythons) were to co-host this nationally networked ABC TV morning show.

At 7.00 the show began, hosted by a lady called Stephanie something or other, an attractive redhead, with a cool, head-of-school-like assurance, but she was playing along well with us and, as the credits rolled, they actually exhorted us to wreck the studio.

We took a cab to the offices of Don Rugoff and Cinema 5, the man and the outfit who are distributing our film in the US. Rugoff's voice, like his general physical presence, is rough and untidy. I liked him a lot.

Sunday, April 27th, New York

We were to be at Cinema II on Third Avenue at 11.00 to welcome the first crowds and to give out coconuts as people came out. The phone rang and woke me about 9.40. It was John Goldstone. Could we get down to the cinema as quickly as possible; there had been people queuing since 5.30 a.m., and Rugoff had already opened the film with a special extra 9.30 performance. There was only one way into the cinema and that was through the main entrance – so through the crowds we went.

Rugoff told us we couldn't go out of the theatre, or let ourselves be seen at a window (!) for fear of inciting riots on Third Avenue.

I think he hoped and expected that there would be riots, but we know our audience quite well – they want to be silly, they want to chat, they want to shake hands, they want you to sign the plaster on their broken arms, but generally speaking they don't want to tear us limb from limb.

But they did fill the cinema all day long, and Rugoff was able to claim at the end of the day a house-record take of ten and a half thousand dollars.

Tuesday, May 13th

Eric's new show *Rutland Weekend Television* was on for the first time last night. Quite a milestone for Python – the first TV manifestation of the parting of the ways. Not a world-shattering show, but a very palatable half-hour's TV. I didn't feel that Python was being used. Of course, there were ideas which Eric would not have written without the influence of five years with Python, but it was still very much his work, his show and his particular kind of humour. I enjoyed it, and TG, who was watching with me, felt the same.

Thursday, May 22nd

At 6.00 at the Henshaws' for a Python meeting. Briskly it was decided to set aside Sept/Oct period of 1976 to write a new film and May/June 1977 to film it.

Monday, May 26th

John Goldstone rang to say that the *Grail* has broken records on its opening in Philadelphia and Toronto and that Don Rugoff has plans to transfer it to a new cinema in NY and wants to have a death cart trundled through the streets of NY as an ad. Given Mayor Bearne's reported plans to sack 67,000 city workers in order to meet huge unpaid bills, this may be a public service as well as a publicity stunt.

Tuesday, September 9th, New York

To Sardi's restaurant, where we had a truly appalling meal, but did meet Arthur Cantor, a Broadway impresario with a fine sense of the absurdity of it all. Cantor talks straight and doesn't try to impress. He would like to know if the Pythons are interested in a stage show in New York at the City Center Theater for three weeks starting April 11th, 1976. The theatre is owned by the City of New York; it's old and has an ornate interior and a seating capacity slightly larger than Drury Lane, though it feels equally intimate.

Friday, September 12th

In the afternoon TJ and I go to the BBC for a meeting with Terry Hughes.

The *Tomkinson's Schooldays* scripts arrive with the title 'Michael Palin Special' writ large across them. [This would be a pilot for what became the *Ripping Yarns* series.]

Friday, September 19th

This evening is the first of John Cleese's solo efforts – *Fawlty Towers* – which he's been working on with Connie for over a year. Helen and I were reduced to tear-streaming laughter on one or two occasions. John has used a very straight and conventional light-entertainment format in design, casting, film and general subject, but his own creation, Basil Fawlty, rises above all this to heights of manic extraordinariness. It all has the Cleese hallmark of careful, thoughtful, well-planned technical excellence.

Thursday, September 25th

Down to Regent's Park for a Python meeting.

Eric was very positive, and I could scarcely believe that it was the same Eric who had berated us all for turning Python into a money-obsessed, capitalist waste of time in this same room in February last year. Eric's moods should really be ignored, but it's impossible because he nearly always has a big effect on any meeting. Today it was nice, kind, helpful, constructive Eric.

Tuesday, September 30th

Had a drink at The Sun in Splendour, Notting Hill with Terry J. He is a little vague and not entirely happy about what to do next. For the first time we actually talked about whether he should go and do something on his own. I said I didn't want to drag his heels as well as my own.

Thursday, November 20th

A Python meeting at 22 Park Square East to discuss the New York show in April and to meet A Cantor.

We have a lot of fun deciding on silly names for our US company, or partnership, or whatever it's called. 'Evado-Tax' is the one we all wanted, but Anne really thought there may be problems, as the company is operating on the fringes of legality! So I suggested Paymortax – and so we now have an American company called Pay mortax and McWhirter!

Tuesday, November 25th

Terry comes up after lunch and we go over to Studio 99 in Swiss Cottage to look at the cassette recordings of Python's first ABC compilation.¹ A very cool American voice – the kind we would only use as a send-up – announces, quite seriously, that 'The Wide World of Entertainment presents the Monty Python Show'. It started well, with 'The World's Most Awful Family', which works a treat after the smooth and glossy ABC packaging of the show, but then the cuts begin. The cat-in-the-wall bell-push (a big laugh in the studio) is cut, the man pouring blood all over the doctors is cut after the open ing lines – before the point of the sketch has even begun. In the 'Montgolfier Brothers' the words 'naughty bits' are bleeped out!!

In fact, any reference to bodily function, any slightly risqué word, anything, as Douglas Adams put it, 'to do with life', was sin gle-mindedly expunged.

---

1. ABC, one of the big three American commercial networks, had bought Python's fourth series (without John) and reorganised it into two specials. We had been tipped off that the result was not good and that we should take a look at it.

The cuts which to me seemed the most remarkable were in the 'Neutron' sketch, when I played the US Bombing Commander who had personal odour problems. The character was in, but every appearance was topped and tailed to avoid all reference to his bodily hygiene. As that was the only original and Pythonesque twist to the character, he just came out as a below-average imitation of George C Scott.

Our reaction turned from disbelief and amazement to anger and outrage and eventually resolved into a very clear and simple position. The first step as far as we're concerned is to let as many people in America as possible know that we disassociate ourselves from the ABC sale. It was suggested that we use our 17,000 lawyers to try and put together grounds for an injunction to prevent ABC putting out the second compilation (due in December). However legally unenforceable this may be, at least it's a fair try for a story – 'Python Sues ABC' would be all we'd need.

Friday, December 12th

Anne rings in the evening. Everyone apart from Eric and Graham, who hasn't been contacted, is solidly in favour of legal action – i.e. the injunction against ABC. Ina Lee M has already spent several thousand dollars of our money to take advice as to whether or not our case is strong. She assures us that we will only have to pay $15,000 *if* the case is to be fought and, if we win and they appeal, maybe $20,000 more on the appeal.

Sunday, December 14th

Things are gathering momentum. Just after 10.00 [the] phone rings. It is T Gilliam. He wants me to go with him to the US tomorrow to be present in New York as Python representatives during the injunction action, etc., etc. We would return Wednesday.

Tuesday, December 16th, New York

There is a great deal of interest and sympathy for Python's case. We make short articles on the Television pages of the *New York Times* and *New York Post*. In the *Times* we learnt for the first time that Time–Life had edited the shows in collaboration with ABC – and that several of the cuts had been made by ABC, said a spokesman, because some passages were considered 'inappropriate'.

One slightly ominous note, though – Nancy says the court hearing is on Friday.

Wednesday morning, December 17th, New York

Up to Nancy's office at Buddah where we meet Rick Hertzberg – a good old friend from *The New Yorker*. Rick is not just a good and sympathetic friend – he also, in his *New Yorker* piece earlier this year (welcoming the Python TV series), has the immeasurable skill of being able to quote our material and still make it sound funny.

From Sardi's the Dynamic Duo, the Fighters for Freedom, find themselves in a rather dingy doorway next to Cartier's shop in Fifth Avenue, waiting for an elevator up to see the lawyers whom Ina has hired to represent us in our struggle against the American Broadcasting Companies, Inc.

They're led by short, blond-haired Robert Osterberg; he must be mid-thirties. A fit, tidy, rather bland sort of man with the eyes and smile, but unfortunately nothing else, of Kirk Douglas.

He begins by saying that we really ought to be in court on Friday. He says, quite rightly, that if no Pythons are prepared to be in New York to defend their own case, that case is immeasurably weakened. And so on. He's right, of course, but both Terry and I have avoided confronting the awful, stomach-gripping truth that we will actually have to defend our position in a US Federal Court.

Thursday, December 18th, New York

A visit to the lawyers, then all of us in a deadly accusing phalanx – Ina, Osterberg plus one, Terry G and myself – make our way over to ABC TV.

Up to twenty-first floor.

We're at ABC today because they yesterday relented their earlier decision not to let us see the proposed December 26th compilation – and the lawyers regard this viewing today as a significant concession.

We meet, for the first time, the highly plausible and eligible Bob Shanks, who is Head of Night Time and Early Morning

Programming at ABC. Intelligent, charming and the man ultimately responsible for our being in New York today. With him is a member of their legal department – a lady in her late thirties, early forties with a long-suffering look in her eyes and a kindly, almost saintly face, as in a sixteenth-century religious painting.

At this stage it's smiles, handshakes, genial informality as far as we're concerned – but for Ina and Bob Osterberg detached cool politeness is the order of the day.

ABC at this point present us with a list of their cuts in the three shows we are about to see. A cursory glance at the list shows that our trip to New York has not been wasted. There are thirty-two proposed cuts. Some ludicrous – 'damn' cut out twice, 'bitch' as describing a dog cut out, etc., etc.

I think that ABC were quite honestly taken aback by our reaction. I just wanted to walk out, but Osterberg advised us to see all the shows, which was obviously good sense.

Next to me on the couch as I told them that the cuts they suggested were totally unacceptable and, in our opinion, ludicrous, was a young, short-haired, conventionally handsome executive, whose eyes would not look at ours for long, and whose face was flushed with confusion. He turned out to be the head of ABC TV's Standards and Practices Department and a Vice-President of the Company.

This was the man whom ABC pay to censor their programmes – the man who had actually decided that the American public wasn't ready for 'naughty bits' – the man who had decided that Eric Idle as Brian Clough dressed as Queen Victoria was a homosexual reference and should therefore be cut. Judging by the list he had compiled, one would expect him to be a sort of obsessive religious maniac.

But the deceit is that of course he was himself no more offended by these words than I am. He laughed, as they all laughed, when we talked about cutting a 'tit' here and a 'tit' there – and yet he will not permit others in his country to have the choice of laughing at those words as well. 'It's alright for us, but we've got to think about people in the South – in Baton Rouge and Iowa as well.' Then we tell him that Python has been running in Baton Rouge and Iowa for over a year on PBS, without complaint.

It all seems so pointless, in this little viewing room in a comfortable office block with a group of people playing idiotic games with each other, but then I remember the power of ABC – the ability to beam a show simultaneously into all the sets in the USA. The papers we have talked to, the radio shows we have talked to, can never hope to reach anything but a small proportion of the audience our mutilated show can reach via ABC.

Our lawyers play games – their lawyers play games. After viewing all the shows we begin sort of negotiations. This involves a worried lady lawyer for ABC asking us if we would ever consider the possibility of re-editing. Yes, we say, despite the obvious harm the ninety-minute format and the commercial breaks will do, we would consider re-editing. Their ears prick up. Our re-editing would be based entirely on artistic and comedic criteria. If in the course of *our* cutting some of their censored words were lost, then fair enough.

'Are there any cuts which we propose,' she says, 'that you would agree with?' 'No', we say. 'It's easier for us to tell you cuts on which we will *never* negotiate and you can work backwards from there.' We single eight points out of the first twelve on which we are immovable.

Much to ing and fro-ing. The lady and the zombie reappear. Yes… there could be some negotiation, but first can we tell them the points in the two other shows which we would be prepared to talk over. Here Osterberg starts to play the impatience game. And quite rightly. He insists, on behalf of his clients, of course, that ABC must first agree to restore all the eight cuts which we regard as non-negotiable. And here they baulk, and the lady lawyer looks more and more desperate, and the zombie walks out and leaves her to us, just as Shanks has earlier ditched him.

Osterberg orders us to put our coats on and we make our way across the heavy, soft carpet, past the clean, neat white desks, with their clean, neat white telephones, towards the elevators. The lady lawyer implores us to keep talking. 'I've been asked to settle this,' she pleads, her eyes moistening with what I would say was genuine fear – whether of us or of her superiors I don't know. Terry G and I smile sheepishly, and the elevator doors close.

Over to the Stage Deli for lunch to restore our sense of proportion. Thank goodness we have each other to compare notes with. I like TG because he is very sane, very realistic, entirely down-to-earth. A couple of waitresses ask us for autographs. They'd loved the *Holy Grail*.

Back to the lawyers later. A gruelling and concentrated working-over of our testimony for two hours, followed by further rehearsals and a taste of cross-questioning.

It was decided that Nancy L should be our first witness in court, followed by myself – through whom Osterberg would bring out all the salient points of our testimony – followed by Terry G, who would weigh in with lavish doses of enthusiasm, conviction and generally play the bruised artist.

Ray, Bob Osterberg's junior, gave me some sample cross-questioning. Although I knew full well it was just a rehearsal, I couldn't help getting thoroughly riled by his techniques of incredulousness, heavy sarcasm, and downright mocking misrepresentation. All – he assured me afterwards – perfectly permissible legal techniques for breaking down witnesses. All I can say is, they worked. I left the office around 11.00 feeling tired, depressed and angry.

Friday, December 19th, New York

At first glance the courtroom was softer, warmer and far less intimidating than I expected. As plaintiffs in the case, we were allowed to sit with our lawyers at a vast and solid table in the front of the court, with the judge's box raised about four or five feet above us, and between him and us the enclosure for the clerks of the court and the court recorders. On our left the jury box, empty of course. Behind the jury box a line of tall windows brightened the court. Immediately behind us the ABC lawyers' table and then, at the back, about a dozen rows of wooden benches for spectators.

The hearing began with the entry of the judge behind a clerk of the court, who was not the old and wrinkled be-robed gent I had expected, but a young casually dressed, Brooklyn-accented, probably Jewish, twenty to twenty-five-year-old girl.

The Judge, Morris Lasker, was not robed either. I wondered whether or not he had seen the Python show which went out in New York on PBS last night, which contained a sketch about a judges' beauty contest!

Nancy testified first – speaking softly and looking composed, but endearingly vulnerable. The Judge was correspondingly gentle with her. He was a honey-voiced, sensible, straightforward sort of fellow, anxious it seemed to avoid long legal discussions. As he said, he had read and studied the legal side of the case – today he wanted to hear witnesses.

It was quite comfortable in the witness box – there was a chair, which I hadn't expected, and I was on the same level as the Judge which helped to put me at ease. As with Nancy, he was kindly throughout my evidence and cross-examination, repeatedly over-ruling ABC lawyer Clarence Fried's objections. I was not grilled particularly hard by Mr Fried. He wasn't anywhere near as aggressive or sardonic or incredulous as I had anticipated from the cross-questioning rehearsal last night.

The most difficult bit was having to describe sketches to the court which had been cut and make them sound funny.

One of the ABC-mutilated sketches which I had to describe to the court actually involved a fictional courtroom, in which an army deserter is being tried before a judge who is constantly interrupting with highly detailed queries. At one point the judge is particularly persistent about a pair of 'special' gaiters worn by the deserter.

What made the gaiters 'special' asks the judge?

'They were given him as a token of thanks by the regiment,' replies the prosecutor.

The judge asks why.

'Because, m'lud, he made them happy. In little ways.'

'In which little ways did he make them happy?' persists the judge.

At this point a bizarre situation became truly surreal as the prosecutor in the real court interrupted me and addressed the judge, in the real court. The following exchange is from the official transcripts:

'Mr Fried: Your honor, this is very amusing and interesting, but I think it is off the track.

'The Court (Judge Lasker): Mr Palin is trying to tell me what the original was like so he can tell me what the effect of the excision will be. Overruled. Go ahead. I am not sitting here just because I am amused, although I am amused.'

Terry Gilliam testified after me. From where I was he sounded very straight, honest and direct. A real all-American boy.

Then, despite attempts from ABC's lawyer to put it off, the really damning evidence was produced. A colour TV was wheeled in and the Judge, and as many as could squeeze in around him, took their places in the jury box to watch two tapes. The first was Show 3 of the fourth series of Monty Python – as it was shown on the BBC. A good show, with the 'Court Martial', 'Gorn' and 'RAF Banter' sketches in it. It went down well. The court recorder chuckled a great deal, as did the Judge and the people operating the TV recorder. Definitely a success. Then was shown the ABC version of the same show.

The ABC version contained long gaps of blank screen where the commercials would go. Three such major breaks in the course of half an hour. The effect on the audience was obvious. It was the end of a very good morning for us.

After lunch, Fried began to call his witnesses. A Mr Burns of ABC's Contracts Department spoke laboriously and with infinite, finely tuned dullness about the possible loss of money caused if the show was cancelled.

Shanks was next. He turned on a bravura display of ingratiating smugness. Oh, he'd been a writer in his time, he grinned. He knew the problems… goddammit, he wouldn't like to lose a line of his own material… but… (Could this be the same man who was quite prepared to authorise the excision of twenty-two minutes out of ninety minutes of Python material? Talk of not wanting to lose a line – we were losing one line in every four!)

Fried bored the pants off everyone with heavy-jowled witnesses from Time-Life who all looked as if they were concealing mass-murders. But a jarring note was struck at the end of the day when a lady at ABC testified that Ina Lee Meibach had rung her on December 10th and had told her that we were not only going to sue ABC, but we were going to drag their names through the mud and squeeze every last ounce of publicity from their predicament. For the first time in the entire proceedings we suddenly felt bad. We were found to be using distasteful, though doubtless common, tactics, and I think it reflects a serious weakness on Ina's part. She is sometimes *too* tough – she takes firmness to the point of vindictiveness.

At 5.00, as it darkened out in Foley Square, the Judge finally withdrew. He reappeared a half-hour or so later and delivered an impressively fluent summing-up which began by raising our hopes at the plaintiffs' table.

He found that ABC's cuts were very major and destroyed an important element of Python's appeal. He found our material was irreparably damaged. My heart leapt. 'But,' he went on to say that he could not grant the injunction for two reasons. One was that the BBC owned the copyright of the tapes sold to ABC, so the BBC should really have been in court too. He was disturbed by the delay in our proceeding against ABC and had to take into account the amount of damage to ABC by our proceeding against them less than one week from the transmission date. So... ABC were off the hook. We'd tilted at windmills and lost.

'But...' Lasker, with a fine sense of timing, had one more twist for us... because of the nature of the damage to us, he would look very favourably on any disclaimer the Pythons would like to put in front of the show when it went out on December 26th. There he finished – and our hopes were raised again. A disclaimer could be as strong and effective as a total ban on the show. Everyone would see us blame ABC openly.

Typical of ABC's extraordinary lack of understanding was that, following this verdict, they approached Terry G and suggested we work out a jokey little disclaimer together!

Out in Foley Square about 6.15. The cold, sub-zero wind whipping around us as we search for a subway entrance. A dark-coated, pipe-smoking figure, head bent down against the wind, crosses the square towards us. It's none other than Judge Lasker. He shows we three frozen plaintiffs the subway and walks down there with us. Alas we have no tokens for the barrier. The Judge scrabbles around in his pockets, but can only find two to give us. Give me the money, he suggests, and he'll go through the barrier, buy us some tokens from the kiosk on the other side and hand them through to us.

We travelled, strap-hanging, with the Judge, up to Grand Central Station. The nearest he got to talking about the case was when Terry G voiced his worries that the existence and the modus vivendi of the Standards and Practices Department of ABC was never questioned, and surely should have been. Yes, said Lasker, he too was worried about the Standards and Practices Department.

He merged into the crowds at Grand Central, and we packed our bags and stretched out in an enormous limousine which bore us from the rather pretty Christmas atmosphere of New York away out to JFK yet again.

Monday, December 22nd

Further news of Python's ever-increasing international status – some fine reviews for *Holy Grail* in France. '*Mieux que* Mel Brooks' – that sort of thing – and the film has apparently opened at a fourth cinema in Paris.

Wednesday, December 24th, Abbotsley

Terry Gilliam rang up to say that, after Judge Lasker had accepted, with minor alterations, our disclaimer for the front of ABC's Boxing Day Special, ABC had appealed, on Monday afternoon, to three other judges, who had overruled his decision. All that will appear are the words 'Edited for television by ABC'.[1]

So, in terms of actual tangible legal rewards for our week in New York and the $15,000 of Python money spent on the case, we were left with very little. I wait to see evidence of the non-legal rewards, in terms of press coverage, etc., etc., before totally writing off our trip, but today's news was a pretty nasty Christmas present.

1. We had wanted: 'The members of Monty Python wish to dissociate themselves from this programme, which is a compilation of their shows edited by ABC without their approval.'

Live stage show in New York;
early discussions of the third film:
Life of Brian;
Live at City Center record album
(January–September 1976)

1976

Friday, January 2nd, 1976

A very cordial Python meeting at Park Square East to discuss the content of our stage show in New York. Once again proved that Python works well as a group when discussing the creation of sketches and jokes – the reason, after all, why we originally got together. Python group at its worst discussing business, contracts, hiring and firing personnel, and other areas which we are better at making fun of than taking seriously.

Today, 'Blackmail' was added to the list, John having said that, although he may be sounding rather selfish, he wanted to cut down the number of sketches he appeared in, and he felt that I was very light in number of appearances. So 'Michael Miles' out and 'Blackmail' in. Graham protested briefly, but the general consensus was that 'Cocktail Bar' should go, along with the 'Bruces' and the 'Pepperpots' in a big purge of the generally accepted weak middle of the first half. In went 'Salvation Fuzz' (entirely new to stage), 'Crunchy Frog' (ditto) – with Graham taking John's role as Inspector Praline – and an amalgamation of court sketches to replace 'Silly Elections' as a closer.

Thursday, January 8th

Gradually dawns on me during the day that *Tomkinson* [the pilot for the *Ripping Yarns* series shown on January 7th] has been something of a success. Jimmy Gilbert rang to give the official BBC verdict. He wants me to go in next Monday and talk about more shows.

Friday, January 16th

Anne had had quite a traumatic meeting this afternoon with Arthur Cantor and Jim Beach[1] to try and finalise the Live Show deal for New York. Cantor is a cautious, kindly theatre producer and is temperamentally quite unsuited to the world of big advances, limousines, $75,000-worth of publicity – which Nancy and Ina's people have been insisting on. So now Anne is having to fix up Allen Tinkley (another American producer).

Thursday, February 5th

A Grammy Award Nomination arrives in the post from LA. *Matching Tie and Handkerchief* has been nominated for Best Comedy Album of the Year.

Tuesday, April 6th, New York

Sunshine in New York and a freshness in the air – a perfect spring afternoon. First sight of our home for the next four weeks, our very own brownstone in East 49th Street, between Second and Third Avenue, No. 242.[2]

Thursday, April 8th, New York

A twenty-five-minute walk across town to our rehearsal room near Broadway. Big, functional, mirrored rehearsal room. Bad news of the day is that Eric has been ill in bed since yesterday.

Wednesday, April 14th, New York

One of those totally gruelling days that only happen in the theatre and, if they didn't have to happen, the theatre would invent them. Eric came in – he's all right.

    10.00 into the theatre. An a.m. technical stagger-through, topping and tailing.

    In the afternoon, a dress rehearsal. Our first and only, despite Hazel's usual protestations. One thing that irritates me about the

---

1. Our legal adviser at the time. Later manager of Queen.
2. I shared the house with Terry J – and later, our families.

afternoon run, which is so important to us, is that we have not been warned that the press has been allowed in.

At 8.00, almost punctually, the curtain rose to prolonged applause and cheers.

The whole show went predictably well, with very few problems and the usual reaction of ecstatic recognition of sketches. I think we're in for an enjoyable run.

Thursday, April 15th, New York

In late afternoon, TJ and I have to go to a reception being given by the BBC. A couple of gin and tonics, and the good news that we have a rave review from Clive Barnes of the *NY Times*. The review, out tomorrow, was circulating the party, as was its author – small, owl-like doyen of NY theatre critics – Clive B himself. He said how much he'd enjoyed it. I went over some of the things that had gone wrong – e.g. the till not working in 'Blackmail' – he said that sort of thing made the show even more fun.

After tonight's show another party – this time quite a cheery affair thrown by Arista in the New York Experience – an exhibition in the bowels of the Rockefeller Centre. A breathless PR lady rushes up and asks me to come and have my photo taken with Leonard Bernstein. The flashbulbs go crazy. As I talk to Lenny I'm actually being pulled to one side by this wretched PR lady so that I don't spoil the shot by obscuring his face from the cameras. He goes on about how he and his kids adore the show. Later he asks John and Eric to do bits of sketches and Eric replies by demanding that Bernstein sing a bit of Beethoven.

Saturday, April 17th, New York

Two shows tonight: 6.00 and 9.30.

At the first show someone is letting off firecrackers very irritatingly. It comes to a head in 'Argument', in which a crack completely obscures a line and Graham leaps in, doing his favourite bit, shouting – or rather, yelling – at hecklers. As he's just done the Man Who Gives Abuse, it all fits in very neatly. The offender is seen to be removed forcibly from the theatre by Jim Beach. G's volley of abuse follows him right up the aisle. The sketch goes swimmingly after that.

Sunday, April 18th, New York

Crowds outside stage door now number forty or fifty. Much screaming and autograph-signing. Nothing like this in London. It's quite
nice for a while. Am given two beautiful Gumbys – one made in
plaster, and another elaborately and painstakingly embroidered –
plus flowers, etc. TJ is given a flower for every performance by one
fan.

Tuesday, April 20th, New York

At the show tonight George Harrison fulfils what he calls a lifetime's
ambition and comes on as one of the Mountie chorus in the 'Lumberjack Song'. He's very modest about it, wears his hat pulled well
down and refuses to appear in the curtain call.

Wednesday, April 28th, New York

At 11.00 all the Pythons, bar Terry Gilliam who is giving a court
deposition, arrive at 242 for the first meeting/discussion about the
next Python movie.

   Are we or are we not going to do a life of Christ? All feel that we
cannot just take the Bible story and parody or Pythonise every well-
known event. We have to have a more subtle approach and, in a
sense, a more serious approach. We have to be sure of our own attitudes towards Christ, the Scriptures, beliefs in general, and not just
skate through being silly.

   John provides a key thought with a suggested title – 'The
Gospel According to St Brian' – and from that stem many improvised ideas about this character who was contemporary with Jesus
– a sort of stock Python bank clerk, or tax official, who records
everything, but always too late – things have always happened when
he eventually comes on the scene. He's a bit of a fixer too, and typical of St Brian is the scene where he's on the beach, arranging
cheap rentals for a fishing boat, whilst, in the back of shot, behind
him, Christ walks across frame on the water. St Brian turns, but it's
too late.

   So at the meeting, which breaks up around 1.00, we seem to have
quite unanimously cheerfully agreed to do a film, and a Bible story

film, and have had enough initial ideas to fill all of us with a sort of enthusiasm which has been missing in Python for at least a couple of years.

Thursday, April 29th, New York

A less productive film meeting at 242 this morning, although we take the Bible story into wider areas, Rome perhaps or even the present day. A silly World War I opening is suggested, which starts with a congregation of English soldiers singing in some chapel. A moving scene. Except in one row at the back there are four Germans singing. Nobody likes to look at them directly, but heads begin to turn.

Monday, May 3rd, New York

A record-signing had been laid on at Sam Goody's Store from 12.00–2.00. Through the traffic, on the opposite side of the road, a queue half a block long. And they're waiting for us. With an increased confidence in our stride we cross the road. A few screams and shouts and we're into the store. The entire basement is full of Python records. The album *Live at City Center* has been marketed in only ten days since the master was cut. There they are. Racks of them.

Thursday, June 17th

Down to Regent's Park for a Python Annual General Meeting. We have three companies – Python Productions Ltd, Python (Monty) Pictures Ltd and Kay-Gee-Bee Music Ltd. We manage to go through the official convening and closing procedure of all three companies in four minutes!

Terry J models the Python T-shirt, which is approved, with a few design alterations.

Finally we agree to spend £30,000 on acquiring full rights from Bavaria TV to the two German specials.

Friday, July 9th

Anne brings me a copy of the Federal Court of Appeals Judgement in the Python v ABC case. The Judgement was dated June 30th 1976 and is very strongly favourable to Python – they recommend that the injunction should be upheld. So Terry's and my trip, in that cold and bleak December (which seems light years away now), was worthwhile after all.

The Judgement indicates that, in the judges' opinion, Python would have a substantial chance of a favourable verdict in the courts and damages and all else that could follow.

I personally am against a big damages award – it may be the way lawyers play it, but I think that the popular image of Python winning $1 million would erase in people's minds some of the reasons why we won it. But I think we should have a strong bargaining counter in any attempt to recover our costs. We shall see.

Saturday, August 21st

[While on the set with Terry Gilliam, filming *Jabberwocky*,] we talked a little about Python and the next movie. TG said he reckoned the film was TJ's to direct – he'd far rather be directing another film of his own.

Tuesday, August 24th

Eric (complete with specially printed T-shirt '*Jabberwocky* – The New Python Movie') came to see us on set. Eric brought me a signed advance copy of the book, *The Rutland Dirty Weekend Book* (containing three pages by M. Palin!), to be released next month. It's a lavish production job – a combination of the Goodies and Python book designs over the last four years, but fused and improved.

Tuesday, September 28th

Visit Anne Henshaw. She has her head down in the labyrinthine affairs of Python as usual. She reports that the sooner we start writing the Python film, the better for some in the group – she says Graham especially seems to be at a loose end and drinking more, with several of his projects, TV series and his film of Bernard McKenna's script, having collapsed. [Graham collaborated with writer and actor, Bernard McKenna, to make the film *The Odd Job*, ultimately filmed and released in 1978.]

12

Writing the third film:
Life of Brian;
publication of
Monty Python and the Holy Grail (*Book*)
(November 1976–September 1977)

1976-1977

Monday, November 8th

The Pythons reassemble at 22 Park Square East for the first day of a two-month writing period on our new film. John suggests straight away that at some point during this writing period we all go abroad to the sun for a week or ten days (to 'really break the back of the film'). This is shelved. As Terry J says, 'Let's all see if we like each other at the end of the day.' But we make plans for the next year – writing until Christmas, rewriting throughout March and filming delayed until September/October 1977. There follows some good chat and exchange of ideas about the story and how to treat it. JC now thinks the film should be called 'Monty Python's Life of Christ'.

Wednesday, November 10th

Writing with Terry – some hopeful starts, but nothing great as yet, the most promising being a piece Terry has begun about the Three Wise Men, confused over which star they're following and being constantly mistaken for the wrong sort of astrologers and having to tell people about their star sign. In the classic Python mould of the humour of frustration; irritation at constantly being diverted by trivia.

Friday, November 12th

Python meeting at Park Square East at ten. All there except TG. Anne sits in (having asked if we didn't mind). All rather institutional. It falls to Palin to start the ball rolling and read the first new, all-Python material since we wrote the *Holy Grail*.

Enough good material from everybody to suggest things haven't changed. In fact, in John and Graham's case, I think they've improved. They wrote the stoning section and an ex-leper and psychopath section – both of which were back on their best form. Very funny.

Anne supplies lunch – prawns and smoked salmon and no booze, except for GC who seems to find a G and T from somewhere. He is on fine form and really elated by his writing week with John.

Wednesday, November 17th

Film writing with Terry. He's still not producing much – but today we have a good readthrough and work on with the Three Wise Men.

Thursday, November 18th

A writing meeting of all the team this afternoon. John and Graham had written little and were not as pleased with themselves as before. Eric had done more thinking than writing – whereas Palin and Jones had produced a mighty wodge of at least twenty-five minutes of material. So reading was not made easier by the fact that there was a total imbalance of contributors. Fortunately Terry Gilliam had taken time off from editing [*Jabberwocky*] at Shepperton to be at the meeting, and his generous and noisy laughter helped a great deal and, by the end, we'd acquitted ourselves quite respectably.

The sketches, or fragments, which work least well at the moment are those which deal *directly* with the events or characters described in the Gospels. I wrote a sketch about Lazarus going to the doctor's with 'post-death depression', which, as I read it, sounded as pat and neat and predictable as a bad university-revue sketch. The same fate befell John and G's sketch about Joseph trying to tell his mates how his son Jesus was conceived. The way the material is developing it looks as though the peripheral world is the most rewarding, with Jesus unseen and largely unheard, though occasionally in the background.

John and Graham are troubled by the lack of a storyline. At the moment, after only about seven or eight days' writing, I feel it's the least of our worries and that we should carry on writing and stockpiling funny material to be fitted into a storyline later. 'But we only have another thirty-two and a half days' writing, little plum,' says John, consulting his diary.

Wednesday, November 24th

A good, workmanlike Python meeting. John and G have a good idea for a *Brian* storyline and their two new pieces, though short, are not just on the point, but very funny – writing 'Go Home Romans' on the wall is going to be a little classic. I wish I'd thought of such a neat idea.

From 22 Park Square East we all (except Gilliam) pile into John's Rolls and purr down to Audley Street, Mayfair, for a viewing of selected Biblical epics, which we feel we ought to see. This viewing theatre at Hemdale is very comfortable, which is just as well as the films – *Barabbas*, *King of Kings*, *The Greatest Story Ever Told* and *Ben Hur* (we see bits of each) – are extremely heavy and turgid. Best performances and best writing always centre on the baddies – Herod, Pilate, etc. – and the nearer you get to Jesus the more oppressive becomes the cloying tone of reverence. Everyone talks slower and slower, and Jesus generally comes out of it all as the world's dullest man, with about as much charisma as a bollard.

We had a few good ideas during the viewing (midst much silly giggling and laughter). I suggested we should have four Wise Men – the fourth one being continually shut up by the others, who always refer to themselves as the Three Wise Men. '*Four*.' 'Ssh!'

Wednesday, December 8th

A Python writing meeting in the afternoon. Quite substantial chunks of material from everyone – including a neat and funny bit by Eric with a magnificent creation – a Jewish Hitler called Otto the Nazarene, who wants more Lebensraum for the Jews.

Is it paranoia, or did I detect a sort of wariness of Palin/Jones material? Our stuff was received well, but both John and Eric unable to accept anything without qualifying their approval – and there also seemed to be a marked resistance to reading all our material.

I think this is partly the fault of late meetings. 2.30 is not the time when everyone is freshest, and by 4.30 Graham was probably right when he said he felt we were 'sated'. We always used to give everything anyone wanted to read a hearing, then throw it away.

Sunday, December 12th

Brief chat with EI, who seems concerned that Terry J should not have too much control of the next Python movie. He does blow hot and cold. It was only a few months ago that Eric wanted TJ to direct his TV series! But now he feels that TJ's problem is that he doesn't appreciate compromise.

Tuesday, December 14th

To 22 Park Square East for an all-day Python session.

Quite a successful meeting. John reckons we have about 40% good material – good meaning strong. I think I'd put it a little higher, though not much. Today we decide on a public-school opening – details of which are improvised at the meeting – and also the rough pattern of Brian's life – a bastard with a Roman father, toys with joining various messiahs, is disillusioned, joins, or dabbles, with the resistance, is caught, escapes from the Romans, disguises himself as a prophet and gains a large and devoted following which he also tries to escape from. John and Graham seem to be keen on using my 'Martyrdom of St Brian' (the soft and luxurious martyrdom) as an ending… but it's on endings we're weakest.

Thursday, December 16th

Almost a year since we went over to defend our reputation in the US Federal Court, we have heard the terms on which ABC are prepared to settle the case, following the successful hearing of our appeal in June. ABC are prepared to pay our legal costs up to $35,000 and are undertaking not to edit any shows without our cooperation and approval. We have established that, should we refuse to edit, the shows cannot go out. From the BBC and Time-Life we have won deadlines within the next five years when the ownership of all the tapes will revert to us.

This was neat justice. The BBC had allowed ABC to make cuts without bothering to consult the Pythons because they didn't consider the American market anywhere near as important as the UK market. So, after US Federal Court judges had deemed this breach of copyright, the BBC were prepared to give us back the rights to all our tapes, so long as they hung on to those for UK TV.

Not only did they still fail to appreciate the growing strength of Python in America, they also failed to predict the burgeoning growth of video and other ancillary rights. Thanks to the BBC's dumbness, sorry, generosity, we were able to negotiate all these valuable rights for ourselves, and the licence payers missed out on quite a few bob.

Tuesday, December 21st

To Park Square East for a final Python reading meeting.

High standard from John and Graham, Eric average and Terry's and my first offering frankly bad. A poor rewrite of a poorly written original is never going to stand much chance before this audience – and it bombs embarrassingly.

A second very encouraging piece from John and Graham – about the crowd outside Brian's home being talked to sharply by Brian's mother.

My personal gloom finally lifted by the reading of our piece about Brian and Ben in the prison and the Centurion who can't pronounce his 'r's. This five- or six-minute piece, read right at the end of the meeting, with both GC and JC poised to leave, really brings the house down. It could be pre-breaking-up hysteria, but it's a good note to end this six-week writing stint.

Wednesday, December 22nd

To the Coronet Viewing Theatre in Wardour Street to see the two Python German TV shows in order that we may finally decide whether to buy them for Python Productions or not.

The first German show, in German, is, apart from 'Silly Olympics' and 'Little Red Riding Hood' and one or two bits of animation, fairly difficult to follow and looks a little rough, whereas the second looks smooth, polished and expensive. John is anti buying them and Eric very pro.

In the end I side with Eric. The money we use to buy the shows would otherwise be taxed very heavily, and I feel that it is a good principle for us to buy the world rights to our work wherever they become available. John agrees, before leaving, to the purchase of the shows (cost around £42,000, largely owing to the strength of the mark and weakness of the pound). Eric agrees to undertake their re-editing.

Friday, March 4th, 1977

Python reassembles. The meeting is at 2 Park Square West, the first time we have met in the Henshaws' sumptuous and very well-appointed new house (on the opposite side of Regent's Park from their previous one).

Eric is there (as usual) already, John arrives shortly after me, then Terry J, and we have to wait for an hour before Graham joins us.

But the general tone of the meeting was of optimistic good humour, stretched almost to the point of hysteria. It was almost impossible *not* to get a laugh. We talked for two to three hours about the script and very silly ideas like a stuffed Pontius Pilate came up. I was in tears on several occasions.

Eric suggests we do our next Python stage show on ice, but don't learn how to skate.

Monday, March 7th

Down to 2 Park Square West. We're all there, TG included, for chats about 'Life of Christ'.

A good ideas session. We talked until four. Cleaned up the ending a good deal. The Centurion who can't pwonounce his 'r's has become quite a leading figure now – in fact, he's probably Pontius Pilate.

Thursday, March 10th

Eric very positive and clearly the one who's done the most work on our two 'separate' days since Monday. He has worked out a putative running order which is a good basis for discussion.

Friday, March 11th

I manage to write some more of the 'Twibune'. Helen suggests he should have a friend, so I write in Biggus Dickus, who thpeakth with a lithp.

Wednesday, March 16th

Slowly begin to overcome some indefinable resistance to writing any new material for the 'Bible' story, and by mid-afternoon I'm beginning to gather momentum. Complete a new 'Headmaster' piece for the opening, then literally race along with an ending montage, pre-crucifixion. The ideas suddenly seem to be released.

Friday, March 18th

Difficult, but finally constructive Python meeting at 2 Park Square West. We assembled at 10.15, but Eric looked unwell, and John did not arrive until ten to eleven.

So neither of those two seemed in the best of moods, and Terry's suggestion that the 'Healed Loony' sketch should open the main bulk of the film (after the 'Nativity') was very sulkily received by John and Eric. The rest of us, including Graham, all remembered liking it and still liked it, but John claims he didn't and Eric doesn't think it's funny enough to start a film with.[1] Terry looks terribly hurt and deflated and says things like it was putting this sketch first that suddenly restored his enthusiasm for the film. But Terry's enthusiasm can work two ways, and it was clearly only hardening John and Eric's attitude today.

Well, fortunately for the meeting, the script and all concerned, we soon got out of this area and began to make some rapid progress with the end, which is now to culminate in a huge crucifixion musical number.

It's interesting to know how people would react. We have de-Jesused the crucifixion, by keeping him out of it (although there were lovely fantasies of him saying to others in the crucifixion procession, 'Oh, do come on, take it seriously'). Instead we have about 150 assorted crooks being led out for crucifixion – which was, after all, a common enough event at that time. But the crucifixion has become such a symbol that it must be one of the areas most sensitive to the taint of historical truth.

---

1. It never did get into the film, but is reproduced in the *Life of Brian* book, along with the 'Headmaster' and other plucky failures.

Wednesday, March 23rd

The Python meeting is very constructive. Eric, who hadn't written much apart from a song, which wasn't that special, was nevertheless on good analytical form, putting his finger time and time again on what was right and wrong with the more sizeable contributions from John C and Graham, and Terry and myself. But we had supplied some good ideas, especially for the end, and the morale of the meeting was high.

We decided that John Goldstone should produce it, and the shooting dates would be January/February/March 1978, abroad. We have given ourselves a three-week writing session in July and a final session in October. We didn't discuss director – I feel that Terry J will do it, unless anyone feels strongly enough against.

Terry J suggests a press ban on discussion of the film. We agree to keep it a secret. John and Eric particularly vociferous about press on set. They just get in the way and do no good. Eric very positive on no deals with censors or producers over language or taste. We and we alone must decide what the final form of the film is to be.

Sunday, March 27th

By this time next week we'll have finished the first real draft of the *Life of Brian*, as Eric suggested calling it on Friday.

Tuesday, March 29th

To Park Square West for a Python writing meeting. A very good session. Our rather hastily written and assembled ending up to the crucifixion reduces people to crawling the floor with laughter. Simple expedients like funny voices finally triumphing over careful intellectual comment.

So all immensely cheered. The film now has an ending – which is something the *Grail* never had – and we seem to have successfully tackled the difficult area of the crucifixion – by treating it all with historical unemotionalism.

Wednesday, March 30th

Morning writing session on Python. Though we work far fewer hours together now, the sessions are becoming more efficient.

Problems once so complex are being solved with a natural ease and unanimity which seemed impossible a year ago. Terry J will almost certainly direct. Gilliam may be in control of design. There is no room as yet for animation.

Friday, April 1st

Much appreciation of a very good *Guardian* April Fool – a seven-page report on a totally fictitious island in the Indian Ocean called San Seriffe. Very well done – complete with photos and adverts and always just on the right side of probability. Eric suggests we send them one of our golden feet (originally made as a present for our US lawyer, Bob Osterberg). Anne is contacted and we send the foot to the *Guardian* 'for services to San Seriffe' on paper headed 'Python Productions Ltd, Evado Tax House, San Seriffe'.

(It's not the first time this week that Python has been moved to feats of appreciation by the newspapers. A *Guardian* report on Monday that *Gay News* are short of £12,000 funds to help them fight the blasphemous libel case brought against them by M Whitehouse for publishing a poem which suggested that Christ received some sexual favours while on the cross, moved us to send £500 as a Python contribution to the mag.)

Monday, July 4th

In the evening, despite terminal drowsiness, I have to read the Python film script, which I haven't touched for three months, and have intelligent comments on it ready for our meeting tomorrow.

Tuesday, July 5th

According to Terry's report (he and TG went location-hunting in mid-June), Tunisia sounds the easiest of the Mediterranean countries to film in. They are well organised, there are good sites and comfortable hotels and the film entrepreneur is the nephew of the President – so no problems stopping the traffic!

But Terry J is not entirely happy with Tunisia – he is worried that we will merely be duplicating all the locations Zeffirelli used, and that it doesn't really look like the Holy Land. John Cleese had had a letter from Israeli Films, trying to persuade us to film there. Terry J wants to look at Jordan. Gilliam says the best hilly city streets are not in Tunisia but in Fez in Morocco, so no solutions are obvious.

Wednesday, July 13th

Some last-minute script work on *Brian*, then drive down to Park Square West for a group meeting. The changes and rewrites to the script are amicably accepted, but we have to agree today on some casting for Friday's readthrough. This casting, whilst it need not be binding for the film, could, as Eric put it, 'stick', so we have to make fairly far-reaching decisions between 12.45 and 1.30 when John has to leave.

Eric tells John (Graham being out of the room) that he, the two Terrys and myself, are of the opinion that John would be wasted as Brian and that Graham might be the best for it – he's Roman-looking, which helps, and was quite good as the central figure in *Grail* – Graham looks good and is watchable.

John erupted at this – far more vehemently than I would have expected. Casting a quick eye at the door in case GC should reappear, he hissed agitatedly that it would be a disaster – take it from John, he'd been working with him recently and he (GC) couldn't even find his place in the script.

Then Graham reappeared and, despite John's outburst, it was suggested to him that he play Brian. Graham mumbled woollily, and we went on to cast the rest – as John had to go. I was given Pilate, Ben, the Ex-Leper and the follower Francis, as well as Nisus Wettus – the centurion in charge of the crucifixion.

Friday, July 15th

Drive over to Primrose Hill for *Life of Brian* recorded script readthrough at Sound Developments.

Talk to John on the way in. I had misjudged exactly how much he *wanted* to play the rather dull central role of Brian. John wants to do a lead, he told me. He wants to have a go at being a Dennis [the 'hero' role Michael Palin played in *Jabberwocky*] because he says it gives him more chance to work closely with the director, to be bound up in the making of the film much more intimately than he was on the *Holy Grail*.

The recording starts well – the studio is spacious and cool and the engineer unfussy. But as the day wears on it's clear that Graham is once again being his own worst enemy. He arrived at ten quite 'relaxed', and has drunk gin throughout the morning. Everyone else is on the ball, but Graham can never find where we are in the script, and we keep constantly having to stop, retake and wait for him. Occasional glimpses of how well he could do Brian, but on the whole his performance bears out every point John ever made.

Monday, July 18th

To Sound Developments at nine to listen, with the rest of the Pythons (bar Eric), to the tape.

We decide to simplify the central section with the raid on Pilate's palace, and cut down on the number of characters – amalgamating a lot of them – and also to shorten the end sequences. General feeling that the first third of the picture is fine.

We split up – Graham and I to write together on the middle section, because John wants to work on the end with either Terry or myself. Given GC's behaviour on Friday at the reading, I don't particularly relish a day's writing with him. I would really rather work on my own.

Friday, July 22nd

Meet Geoffrey Strachan and the marketing man at Methuen to discuss ideas for promoting the new book of the *Holy Grail*. I suggest we should publish our own top-ten list of bestsellers in every ad, and make up specious names like *The Shell Guide to Dead Animals on the Motorway*.

Geoffrey seems highly pleased. [I] walk over to Park Square West for a final Python meeting. Because we only have a little over an hour to make decisions, we work well and extraordinarily productively. No writing again until January – when we shall spend two or three weeks writing and rehearsing. The West Indies is mentioned.

Monday, August 22nd

Jill Foster rang to say that Python had been approached to appear in the Royal Variety Performance this year. She said that, when the gnarled old showbiz pro who puts the show together rang her, he had been rendered practically speechless by the fact that she said she'd ask us and see, but there wasn't a great chance we'd do it.[1]

Friday, September 2nd

A Python meeting at eleven to discuss what needs to be rewritten, if anything, on the *Brian* film script. Because the retyped version only became available yesterday, no one's had much chance to read it, so we fall to talking of dates, budgets, etc.

Tunisia is decided upon for all the filming, so we set aside ten weeks – starting on April 10th (the nearest date after the end of this financial year).

I put my foot down over writing abroad in January *and* March as preparation for the film. However, we agree to meet and write and read and rehearse in the West Indies in January.

We part on good terms – the great thing about arguments over style is that they never really scratch the surface of our personal relations. We all know we need each other and we all agree to differ. So Python winds down until January 1978 in the West Indies. 'See you next term,' shouts Eric, as I disappear into the rain.

1. She was right.

Compilation record album:
*The Monty Python Instant Record
Collection*;
more work writing and casting
Life of Brian
(September 1977–January 1978)

1977–1978

Monday, September 12th

André (Jacquemin) and I listened to his compilation so far of the new Python album material. It sounds rather good – tightly packed Python gems.

Wednesday, September 21st

See Terry G in the evening. He is very enthusiastic about the cover design (the self-forming box) for the new 'Best of' album, which [he] wants to call *The Monty Python Instant Record Collection*. He wants material for the cover – blurb of any kind and lots of false titles for LPs.

Monday, October 17th

Dr Chapman on the phone for the first time in many weeks. To say how worried he is about the content of the *Instant Record Collection*. I grit my teeth, for it is a little late in the day for fellow Pythons to start showing interest in a record they all seemed fairly apathetic towards two months ago. I was left to put it together, and it was mastered last week. But I'm quite happy to go round and talk over the record with him.

Graham, gin and tonic in hand, looks well scrubbed and far more normal than usual. I am able quite easily to talk him out of most of his peripheral worries. GC just seems pleased to have a fellow Python to chat to.

Sunday, November 20th

Ron Devillier, of Dallas, Texas, the man who finally got Monty Python onto American TV, is in town. Ron is now the buyer for the entire PBS network and is based in Washington.

Over lunch he tells the true story of Python in the US. In 1972, Ron was in New York. 'It was raining, and I had nothing to do,' was how he started the tale. So Ron rang Wyn Godley of Time-Life Sales and asked if there was anything at all left for Ron to view. Wyn looked at his lists and said there was a BBC comedy show called Monty Python, but everyone who'd seen it had rejected it. Ron was a little intrigued, and it was a filthy day, so he went over to see it.

It was Monty Python's 'Montreux' episode. Ron liked it. Took a copy back to Dallas, looked again and rang Wyn back to ask if there were any more. Wyn found that there were thirteen tapes available. 'Send 'em all.'

One day, coming into the office at six, Ron sat down and viewed all the tapes. His only problem then, he said, was to avoid racing to the phone or in 'any way letting Time-Life know that I thought they were the greatest things I'd ever seen'.

In the end he controlled his enthusiasm, but still found Time-Life asking $500 each for the right to two showings of each programme. Ron, alone, consulting nobody, wrote out the $6,500 cheque one evening. That was his act of faith.

But the fairytale ending is that the shows were such an immediate success in Dallas that, on the first night an uncut Python show was aired in the US, Ron received more pledges of money to the station than the $6,500 he'd paid for the entire series.

New York got wind of this success and for once the smart East Coast found itself having to follow Texas, but NY paid $2,000 per show. The rest, as they say, is history.

Friday, December 2nd

This morning we have the first meeting of the Pythons to begin the lead-up to the movie which starts, all being well, in April.

John Goldstone addresses us first. John [G], now firmly established as producer of the next movie, wishes us to help him out in raising the loot. [He] virtually rules out private investors, and

Michael White [has said] there is no way he can lay his hands on the money we require – about eight times as much as we were asking for on the *Holy Grail*.

John G says Warners have all read it and loved it (which I can't believe), but a bit of Python flag-waving would not go amiss. To this end he suggests an interview with *Variety*, *Hollywood Reporter* and other magazines which land softly on air-conditioned office desks in Burbank.

Eric is appalled by the idea. (I'll grant Eric that – his attitude to the press is one of the few that has remained consistent over the last five years!) He suggests putting an ad in *Variety* aimed at showing American producers what an extraordinary worldwide force Python is. John [C] suggests a byline – 'You were late for World War One, late for World War Two... Don't be late for...'

The next leading question is where we should rewrite in January. Eric suggests Barbados – I question whether we would actually do any work in Barbados. This consideration doesn't seem to weigh heavily on John or Eric.

The cover of the *Instant Record Collection* was greatly approved of. Thank you, Terry Gilliam (though I don't think anyone got around to saying that).

Thursday, December 15th

We all assemble at Eric's house in Carlton Hill to look at tapes of various ladies we're considering for the Judith part. Judy Loe [in] the cabin scene from 'Curse of the Claw' [one of the *Ripping Yarns*] goes down well, John falling about especially loudly, which was gratifying. Penny Wilton's *Norman Conquests* performance goes down well. The final list is Judy Loe, Penelope Wilton, Maureen Lipman, Diana Quick and Gwen Taylor – and we decide to arrange a readthrough with them all as soon as possible.

Saw a glimpse of *All You Need is Cash* [Eric Idle's Beatles parody]. It was impressive – well paced and well shot and with some very funny performances by such as Neil Innes. John needed persuading that Neil could act. The rest of us are unanimously pro-Neil for the film, but there are quite strong differences of opinion as to who and how many we need for the supporting repertory cast in

Tunisia. Good company is considered by all to be a major require-
ment, and some of the names bandied are Roger McGough, Ken
Colley and Terry Bayler (from *All You Need is Cash*).

Friday, December 16th

I buy the *Melody Maker*, which contains something of a landmark
in Python history – the most comprehensive, overt piece of mud-
slinging yet seen in public from one of the group. Wild, angry and
drunk, Graham at last says what he feels about the *Ripping Yarns*
and the various Pythons. I must admit I laughed greatly when I
read it – at GC's drunken audacity, which makes for brighter reading matter than most of our interviews. Oh, well, GC once again
spices our life up – it's a pity he had to spice it up with such mis-
anthropic stuff.

Thursday, December 22nd

The auditions [for the part of Judith] were pleasant, easy and pre-
Christmassy. Maureen Lipman, surprisingly, seemed to find it hard
to become a character, but she's nice and fun. Then Diana Quick,
exuding confidence, swept the place with a devastatingly assertive,
aggressive reading of Judith, which confirmed Terry J's suspicion
that Diana, just being Diana, was the sort of character Judith should
be. Judy Loe was not as forceful, and a little pantomimey.
     As John C put it afterwards, he rated both Judy and Maureen as
lovely, easy, friendly people whom we'd obviously have no trouble in
fitting in with, and vice versa, but Diana Quick clearly gave Judith a
new dimension of aggression and single-mindedness, which brought
the limpid part to life. So Quick will be asked to do Judith. If she
does it, she and I will be renewing a working relationship that started
at the Oxford Revue of '65.

Thursday, December 29th

I'm at work today, quite gratefully, going through the text of the *Ripping Yarns* down at Methuen.
     Home and Helen says to me, rather gravely, 'Well… Graham
Chapman…'

My first instinct is to ask if he's dead, but he's not, of course, although he is in hospital, having collapsed at home after four days off the bottle altogether. He rings me later, and sounds small, weak and very old. He confirmed the story. He added that it was remorse for the nasty things he's been quoted as saying in newspaper [interviews] recently about all the rest of us that shocked him into giving up.

'... I tell you one thing, Mikey, I'm never going to drink strong drink again' (and he sounded as if he meant it).

Sunday, January 1st, 1978

John rings. He's been away in the country for the weekend. Has just returned to find a message that Graham has had a nervous break-down. John admits that at first he saw it as just another Chapman wheeze to avoid the stick which would inevitably fly in Barbados over his newspaper interviews. Not far off the truth, John.

Tuesday, January 3rd

Dropped in to see Graham in Southwood Lane. He came out of hos-pital yesterday and is not supposed to drink ever again. It's going to be a great struggle for him.

Further work on writing,
financing and casting
Life of Brian
(January–September 1978)

1978

Saturday, January 7th, Barbados

We reached Barbados an hour before sunset. Our way wound up the west coast of the island and from Bridgetown north it was a dense collection of hotels, shops, clubs, some discreetly set away behind shrubberies and palm groves.

Down one such turning is Heron Bay, built by Sir Ronald Tree. Its scale is breathtaking – wrought-iron gates, marble floors, piano nobiles – the full Palladian bit. All built in 1947. John spreads himself across a huge, soft, cushion-filled sofa and declares 'This is what my whole life has been leading up to.' Churchill has stayed here and there's a photo of Eden and signed photos of impressive-looking men in medals and uniforms.

Sunday, January 8th, Barbados

Graham is stoutly and very worthily maintaining his non-drinking, helped by a pill called Herminevrin. Talking with Eric and Graham in the front row of the stalls at sunset – when the sky and the bay go through so many rich colour changes in half an hour – Graham suddenly asks me the date. When I tell him it's the 8th he murmurs with ruminative interest… 'Mm… It's my birthday.' So we toast GC's thirty-seven years in fruit juice.

Monday, January 9th, Barbados

We fairly roar through the script and there's a very productive feeling that at this stage anything is worthy of discussion. We are not under pressure, everyone is warm, comfortable, happy, looking forward to a swim and sunbathe, and therefore amazingly tolerant of any ideas, however devious, deadly or heretical. The script is being turned upside down and inside out.

More work in the afternoon, but we break after one and a half hours to take in the sunset. I think I could cross my heart and say that we did work hard today, with Anthony Eden surveying us urbanely from his signed photograph.

Tuesday, January 17th, Barbados

Towards the end of last week we began to summarise what we had achieved and this meant going back over well-trodden ground. Ideas, lines and jokes lost their originality and spontaneity and false trails were too laboriously followed. The lightness of touch was lost and the work became harder. But we kept at it successfully, and over the weekend reached the stage where we were to split into separate writing units and begin to actually rewrite along the lines of the five days' discussion.

This morning we had a readthrough of everyone's rewrites. Terry and I may have had the easiest part of the script, but our work was mostly accepted and approved. John and Graham had worked on the second section, which was stretched out painfully in certain areas – Eric reckoned 25% of it was superfluous. John took this well. He has remarked in several beachside chats last week on how unselfish we all are with our material.

Wednesday, January 18th, Barbados

Apart from a break for lunch today, we work assembling the script from 9.45 until 1.00 and 3.30 until 7.30.

And suddenly it's there and ready.

There is now casting, reading-through and minor line rewrites left. John suggests a light day tomorrow, and nobody really argues. We're all feeling rather pleased with ourselves.

Friday, January 20th, Barbados

Casting completed this morning. Most of the main parts reaffirmed. Brian is Graham (unchallenged), Terry J Mandy (John being the only other one in the running, but it was felt that a motherly ratbag was needed, and TJ's women are more motherly than JC's long, thin, strange ones), Eric Otto, me Pilate, and so on.

TJ feels that the Pythons should play as many parts as possible. John C feels we should be able to afford to take really good actors to play supporting parts, but the general consensus is that our rep company should avoid actors, and be composed of people who can act but will, more importantly, be good companions over ten weeks in Tunisia. Neil [Innes] and Bernard McKenna go on to the list.

Saturday, January 21st, Barbados

The sunset was ten out of ten today – as if laying on some special final perfect treat for us to remember the island by. Eric, in his long messianic white robe, strummed his guitar beside a beach fire, with a full moon shining over the Caribbean.

Monday, January 30th

Gather at 12.30 at 2 Park Square West. John Goldstone has news for us. He produces papers which he hands to all of us. Set out in the type-written sheets are the terms of an anonymous offer which looks to provide us with what we were asking for: £1,240,000, which covers our budgeted below-the-line costs, and £512,000 (less than the £600,000 we asked for) for above-the-line. Artistic controls are not required and the terms of finance are 50% of the profit.

So far so good. John G, warming to his theme, gives an impish smile and is very coy about revealing who it's from. 'The National Front?' I asked him. He grins and produces another piece of paper headed with the dread name EMI. So EMI are back. EMI, who turned down *The Holy Grail* – then later picked it up for distribution and produced a pusillanimous campaign which rejected nearly all our ideas.

Now, three years later, we have a memo which reads 'The board have already said it would be scandalous if EMI did not support its own major talent (i.e. Python) and let it go to an American major.' Ho! Ho!

For the volte-face we have to thank the new brooms of Michael Deeley and Barry Spikings, who used to run British Lion, and have now been brought in to zip up EMI's film production.

Tuesday, February 14th

Write a lyric for the Shirley Bassey-style *Brian* song which I want André and Dave [Howman] to have a go at – just to see whether it works. They have a choir at their disposal for a session, and actually asked me if I had anything I wanted them to do.

Wednesday, February 15th

TJ arrived midday for a session. Needless to say it was Python film business which dominated.

We spent a couple of hours on a rewrite for the second Pilate and Brian scene, which benefited, I think, but I'm always wary of duty rewrites – alterations resulting from irritation with other alterations. I tend to think that a lot of final details are best sorted out when we rehearse together.

Sunday, February 26th

André J brings round the tape of the Shirley Bassey-type *Brian* song that they've put together. It sounds stupendous. Massive brass backing and a great female voice. All done by three people and a lot of mixing.

Back home, ring Graham to wish him well for the start of *Odd Job* filming – at Shepperton tomorrow.

Monday, February 27th

To Anne's for a meeting. Played the Bassey *Brian*. Good reaction, especially from JC. All full of admiration for André's arrangement, though not for my lyric particularly. I agree.

Wednesday, March 1st

Am finishing typing a *Telegraph* 'opinion' piece, when a grave S[imon] Albury [television journalist and producer, an old friend] enters the writing sanctum. He's been talking to Barry Spikings, who's been talking to Lord Delfont, who has stopped the EMI/Python deal because he was so outraged by the script.

My immediate reaction is a surge of relief, spreading to all parts of the body. Confirmation of fears that I had pushed back into my subconscious that EMI would 'find us out' at some stage and get cold feet.

Thursday, March 2nd

John Goldstone calls. The facts are correct. Michael Carreras[1] showed the script to Delfont, who vetoed it. Spikings, however, has undertaken to provide us with £50,000 to keep our production team together whilst we find new backing.

Friday, March 3rd

Evidently none of the Pythons is distraught over the collapse of the EMI offer. Terry J greatly relieved that Python still has its powers of aggravation. EMI are the black-tie gala luncheon, awards dinners establishment – the Grades and the Delfonts of this world – and no territory is less familiar or acceptable to us than this chummy world of showbiz conformists.

Monday, March 6th

JC rings with comments on the rewritten *Brian* ending. Generally he finds it an acceptable and much-improved replacement, but there are one or two points – like the stammering Gaoler – which he has always disliked, and when he turns the full beam of his intellectual logical judgement upon what strikes us as spontaneously funny, it does wither the material. I predict a stubborn confrontation on that scene. But all else constructive.

I now favour a clear decision to avoid the summer and begin *Brian* in autumn, but there are difficulties – costumes are hired, sets in Tunisia are apparently not available in the autumn, etc., etc. Meanwhile, wigs are measured, scripts are rewritten and costumes continue being sewn.

---

1. Film producer, specialising in Hammer horror films, and at the time working for EMI.

Wednesday, March 8th

Gilliam rings for half an hour, proposing a new course of action on the movie – i.e. to cut our budget to a reasonable size by abandoning plans to film in Tunisia, using Britain and finding unusual locations and using a stylised design treatment. The talk turns to castles and salt mines in Wales. 'Jesus of Shepperton', I call this plan.

Monday, March 13th

At 9.30 Python, less Graham, assembles to contemplate the wreckage of the EMI deal. Surprisingly little vindictive comment or post-mortem gloom – though we all feel that EMI should be pressed as hard as is legally possible to provide some recompense for pulling out of a deal after hands were shaken and firm commitments given verbally and literally.

Meanwhile all potential money sources are to be tapped – and Eric suggests that he and J Goldstone go to New York together and try to rifle the pockets of heavily solvent record companies. Anne is to investigate the legal and commercial likelihood of raising the money by shares from the public (fans, etc.). Meanwhile Python (Monty) Pictures is left with a near £70,000 bill to pay for work on *Brian* so far. It looks as though all our income through Python will have to stay there for at least six months.

Sunday, March 26th

Anne rings on Easter morning, no less – with a problem I could well do without. Eric is back, full of *Rutles* success in the US. [His parody of the Beatles started as a sketch on television, then morphed into a record album and a spoof documentary.] He's probably going to edit *All You Need is Cash* film into a seventy-minute version for the cinema, and is strongly urging us to put his forty-minute compilation of the Python Bavaria material out, as a second feature. It would keep Python's name in the American eye whilst we are refinancing *Brian* and would, given the success of *Rutles*, be a sure money-earner.

Apparently the two Terrys and John will hardly consider the idea at all.

Wednesday, March 29th

Eric was rather low I think, because he felt he had tried to do something with the German film and been sat on by the rest of us without even a chance to explain it at a meeting. But I didn't really need to tell him how jealous the Pythons are of each other's material. How ruthlessly and subjectively biased they are against anything which any individual in the group tries to do – and that's probably at the root of their/our unwillingness to throw forty minutes of Python in with the *Rutles*.

Thursday, April 13th

Anne rings with positive news on John Goldstone's meetings with Denis O'Brien,[1] our latest, and probably last, hope for *Brian* backing. Apparently O'Brien has okayed the budget, but is negotiating over above-the-line costs. So *Brian* is on the way to a resurrection.

Friday, April 21st

In the afternoon, drive down to Anne's for a meeting with John Goldstone and the Pythons to discuss the new *Brian* deal.

This has been put together by Denis O'Brien and his company, EuroAtlantic. He will collect £400,000 from four rich folk and then borrow the rest, on their behalf, from the bank. The £2 million borrowed can then be written off against taxes.

Nearly everything we asked for is granted – and they seem less worried about controls than EMI. They *do* want to work closely with John [G] on all distribution deals, and we are being asked to put up £200,000 of our (and John Goldstone's) fees to cover the completion guarantee, and £177,856 of our fees for the contingency money.

If we are all good boys and the weather's nice and there are no revolutions, we will make more money up front than the EMI deal. But if we overrun or overspend then, by the terms of this deal, Python stands to be hit harder.

We talk on for two hours. Eric is aggressive – sometimes quite outrageously awkward over small points – but it's very good to have

---

1. American merchant banker introduced to us by George Harrison. He'd been Peter Sellers' financial adviser.

someone in the group stirring it up, when the rest of us are really happy to accept this stroke of good fortune.

Friday, May 5th

We signed the contract with EuroAtlantic, which gives us £2 million to make the next Python movie.

When Anne asked if there were any points in the contract we wished to discuss, there were unanimous shouts of 'Get on with it!' and 'Give us the money', so the signing went ahead with due irreverence for this vast sum we are acquiring. A magnum of champagne was opened.

At this point Oscar Beuselinck,[1] the lawyer we have approached to help us on the Bernie (Delfont) front, arrives. He sits himself down comfortably and confidently – a marked contrast to most people's behaviour when first confronted by the massed Pythons – as if preparing for a performance.

Oscar clearly relishes the case. In his opinion, Bernie can't take the Otto bit about Jews putting people into 'little camps' – too near the truth about the West Bank, etc.

The upshot of Oscar's jolly visit is that we are, on his advice, going ahead with plans to sue Delfont for the money we had to pay out, and for loss of earnings due to rearrangement of our activities – on the basis that there was an oral contract, and with the moral point that we should do everything legally possible to react against this blatant act of personal censorship as being detrimental us, good business and the British film industry... Amen.

Python has always enjoyed a fight – and with the heads of ABC and Time-Life on a charger already, we're now spoiling for action nearer home.

Thursday, June 8th

TJ tells me Diana Quick can't do Judith in the *Life of Brian*, as she is committed to the RSC in the autumn.

---

1. Much-sought-after entertainment lawyer. Known for ringing up his opponent and saying 'I'm Oscar, what's your best point?'

Friday, June 9th

So TJ, myself and a very much slimmed-down Dr Chapman, meet Sue Jones-Davis. A tiny, boyish little Welsh lady with an upturned nose. Dressed in jeans and shirt – no frills. She reads Judith in a delightful Welsh accent. She's quite a tough and sparky little girl, and has a strong, open face, which should come across well in all the Judith v Brian close-ups. Not a versatile comedy lady like Gwen Taylor, but a good Judith, we all think.

Friday, June 16th

Keith Moon is unanimously voted into the rep company. John Young, the Historian in *Grail*, is unanimously voted in as Matthias, the largest single non-Python role in the movie. We can't agree yet on a Judith.

Eric's two songs – 'Otto' and the 'Look on the Bright Side' crucifixion song – are rather coolly received before lunch.

My suggestion of Ken Colley as Jesus is accepted *nem. com.* – thus solving quite a long-term problem. And the title is to be *Monty Python's Life of Brian* – not 'Brian of Nazareth' as GC and I liked, or 'Monty Python's Brian' as TJ suggested.

Saturday, July 1st

A Python readthrough at Anne's.

A little stilted to start with. Graham has a long list of suggestions and each scene is rather heavily post-mortemed. Then we suddenly find three hours have gone by and Terry J hurries us all through. The state of the script isn't bad, but doubts are voiced about Judith's role (by Terry G) and Brian's. The usual arguments that they're rather dull parts – and as soon as we start to work on the Brian/Judith relationship we lose the comedy.

Indecision still over the casting of Judith. Gwen is good, but I feel Judith needs to be tougher, stronger, more dangerous than Gwen could ever be. We need a stroppy feminist with a sense of humour to play the role.[1]

---

1. After a few more auditions, Sue Jones-Davis was confirmed in the role, and was brilliant.

Sunday, September 10th

This morning's leave-taking [for Tunisia] is easier, emotionally and physically, than some I can remember. An enormous American limousine, of the low, interminably long, black New York variety, swung into [Gospel Oak] Village, and out stepped Dr Chapman in immaculate light-grey suit, and matching it, and creating the final and complete effect of flamboyant elegance – nay, even stardom – was a light-grey fedora. Never, outside of a sketch, have I seen the Doctor looking quite as dashing.

[In the car] Graham and I talked of Keith Moon, who was to have been in the movie and flying out soon to join us, but who died some time on Thursday night, after a party. Graham, whose abstention from alcohol has increased his appeal a hundred per cent – he now sounds like, as well as looks like, a very wise old owl – told me that Keith was trying to cut down his Rabelaisian appetite for booze, and had some pills called Heminevrin to help out, but these should be taken under carefully controlled conditions and never with alcohol. So Keith had just gone too far.

Filming *Life of Brian* in Tunisia
(September–November 1978)

1978

Sunday, September 10th [continued]

A long taxi drive from Tunis to Monastir as night fell. Impressions of aridity, emptiness, scrubland stretching away on either side of the road. A camel train tottering, or rather swaying, in that peculiarly restful camel motion, along a dried-up riverbed.

To the Hotel Meridien by eight. It's large, new and comfortable.

Monday, September 11th, Hotel Meridien, Monastir, Tunisia

Looking through the script, it strikes me, not for the first time, that the schedule is very full indeed. A long and ambitious film to be squeezed into the eight-week shoot we have planned. Can't help but feel that some scenes will be trimmed or cut altogether.

Wednesday, September 13th, Monastir

A phone call from John Goldstone and Terry J to see if I could exert pressure on John C to agree to shooting the stoning sequence on Saturday. Tim Hampton [line producer] had suggested we start two days early as all the crew were here and ready to go, and it would give us an invaluable extra day in the packed schedule.

John stuck to an awkward stance – that we could indeed do the day, but he wasn't going to endanger a 'major' comedy scene like the stoning on a first day. Some sense there. But, as we rehearsed it today, it seemed not only easier to shoot than perhaps we'd feared but, even at this stage, very funny.

Thursday, September 14th, Monastir

Woken at 8.15 by Terry Gilliam who, with a construction team waiting, was anxious to have the latest on whether JC was prepared to do
the stoning scene – for stones and rocks have to be made today. Able
to reassure him.

After rehearsals we go up to the Ribat fortress for a photocall for
a *Variety* ad to herald the start of shooting. Nostalgia time. John was
dressed in his pakamac as Praline,[1] complete with dead parrot. Terry
J had drag on and a huge lipstick smudge across his lower face. Graham C was in his Colonel's outfit – which hangs off him now he's lost
weight! Eric was in spangly jacket, and I was in knotted handkerchief.
And here we were photographed against mosques and palm trees.

Saturday, September 16th, Monastir

The first day of filming.

A decision [was] reached last week that we should start early and
have as much time off as possible in the middle of the day. We have
to finish before six, when we lose the light.

Drove in my little grey Renault 5, along the road across the salt
flats, past Monastir Airport, past Bourguiba's [the then President of
Tunisia] summer palace. Finally turned sharply left in the direction
of the bright, white, elegantly simple and unadorned lines of the
Ribat – and its fake sister building (built by Zeffirelli for *Jesus of
Nazareth*), which stands rather impertinently beside it.

A take has just begun, and John Young, dressed in loincloth, is
being dragged to the stoning yard beneath the outer walls of the
Ribat by a wonderfully dressed, swirling crowd. It's an impressive,
exciting, authentic biblical crowd – and more than anything today
gave me a sharp boost of confidence.

A crowd of ladies in beards has been assembled from a nucleus
of our rep company, Tunisian actresses, Tunisian non-actresses and
several people from Manchester who are on holiday.

John C is a little stiff in his early performances, but loosens up
as he realises it's going to be rather good. John Young is wonderful.
As JC says, though, considering this is the first day of principal

---

1. Mr Praline was the name John gave to his man in the plastic mac.

photography on a 'major motion picture', there's no sense of occasion, we just get on with it. Terry J hops about in a businesslike way, and doesn't exude any of the egomania of the Great Director. Peter Biziou[1] and John Stanier (camera operator on *Midnight Express*) are equally efficient and unflamboyant.

Then later in the afternoon the camera breaks down. Could this become a traditional feature of Python first days?

I change and, while a huge stone is being dropped on John Cleese, go into the Ribat and work over my words for the Pilate scene on Wednesday. Then I sit in the rather calming air-conditioned comfort of the caravan and learn some of the Shepherds scene.

Monday, September 18th, Monastir

Woke early – and tried some Pilate oratory for Wednesday. I can really bellow here, and am happily screaming something like 'This man wanks as high as any in Wome', when, out of the emptiness, a young Arab on a bicycle appears. He cycles, slowly, warily, past me for a moment, then, after he's put in a suitable distance, he takes one last look and cycles off like a man possessed.

Tuesday, September 19th, Monastir

Called today to be Francis crawling through tunnels on the way to capture Pilate's wife. We filmed on until seven.

Graham is rapidly becoming a saint. He's been treating so many people in the unit – and now he's stopped drinking he has time to do his medical work properly, and the ability to do it without shaking or dropping whatever he's about to stick in you. In the evenings Graham does his rounds, with pills and rubs and words of reassurance.

Apart from his medical activities, he's sharp on his words and, from being a rather disconcerting influence on previous Python epics, he's now become a model of cooperation and efficiency, and his avuncular presence is calm and reassuring. In fact, John today suggested that Graham was reminding him more and more of a vicar.

---

1. Director of Photography – also for, among others, *Bugsy Malone*, *Mississippi Burning* and *The Truman Show*.

Wednesday, September 20th, Monastir

Up at six, and on the road to Monastir by six-thirty. My first really testing day – the Pilate forum speech.

The morning goes well, except that it is possibly the hottest, least windy day yet and out on our rostrum it becomes almost unbearable. But we cover everything bar John's close-ups, then bring in the Tunisian crowd, whom we have heard outside the walls of the Ribat learning to shout 'We want Wodewick!'

They are marvellous, and it's a tremendous confidence boost for the rest of the filming, for at one time the difficulties of teaching Python techniques to a crowd of Tunisians seemed almost insuperable. However, today Terry J has this mixed bunch of Arab students, peasants, grandmothers, mothers with babes in arms, old men with missing noses, middle-aged men with almost leprous skin, lying on their backs and waggling their feet in the air. They find no trouble in jeering at the posturings of the Roman Empire, and seem to enjoy it immensely.

I talked yesterday with Mahomet, who is one of our Tunisian extras, and was one of the raiders in the tunnel. He belongs to a theatre group in Mahdia, and much of their work is critical of the status quo in Tunisia. 'Anti-Bourguiba?' I asked. He shushed me quickly. 'You can end up in prison saying things like that.'

Thursday, September 21st, Monastir

Back on our imperial rostrum again this morning.

One of the great delights is playing with John on one of his close-ups. John is, on a good night, one of the world's great corpsers, and today I have the rare luxury of being able to try and corpse him absolutely legitimately. On one take he is unable to speak for almost half a minute.

Friday, September 22nd, Monastir

At the location by eight to provide off-camera lines for the crowd at Mandy's house, which is located in a busy corner of the Ribat, dressed to give the feeling of a Jerusalem tenement block of AD33. Lots of Gilliam detail. Full of Arabs, it really looks amazingly good.

Graham gives us a few full-frontals early on. He does pose rather well – probably an unconscious result of many years' absorption in gay mags.

As well as our ever-enthusiastic crowd of Arabs, we also have some English tourists, rounded up from nearby hotels and referred to by various collective nouns – the 'Clarksons', the 'Cosmos'.

I was asking our patient, hard-working Arab assistant director, who has the unenviable task of explaining Terry's instructions, how the locals were assembled. Apparently some are students and others just villagers, recruited after a tour of the surrounding areas in which the assistant director, as he told me, 'explained Python to them'. That must be worth some sort of award.

Terry J's method of teaching an Arab crowd to speak English is quite a phenomenon... He was pressed for time, admittedly, but the Jones technique went something like this...

'Let's try it then... "We are all individuals".'

The good-natured, completely baffled Arabs mimic Terry as best they can.

Terry: 'Good...! Good... you've nearly got it... Once more, "We are all individuals".'

Arab noise.

Terry: 'Very good... Now let's try, "Yes, we must decide everything for ourselves".'

Economic note: the Arab extras get three dinars per day (£3.50), plus a loaf of bread and a tin of sardines at lunchtime. We are getting about a thousand pounds per filming day, plus accommodation at a first-class hotel and a lunch from the Italian caterers which will be a choice of spaghetti, ravioli, steak, veal, omelette, salad and fresh fruit.

Saturday, September 23rd, Monastir

At the make-up house at seven to prepare for the Ex-Leper. On the set, I realise how much of an ivory tower I am in at the Meridien – and such detachment surely does not behove a diarist. I missed, for instance, the scenes after Pilate's filming. Apparently there were near riots as people struggled to make sure they got their three dinars. On Friday morning, Terry J's car was chased by hopeful extras as he left the hotel.

Monday, September 25th, Monastir

See John C leaving. He says, ominously, that although he's not in today's scenes, he is going to 'help out' behind camera. John Goldstone is worried about TJ's unshakeable commitment to full-frontals in the Mandy/Brian bedroom scene. Says he's talked to John about it. So that's why John's gone in.

Arrive on set to find a harassed Terry J. He's not pleased at John's interference today – words have been changed at the last minute. TJ, GC both feel very tensed-up by John's presence 'behind the camera'. The first sign of any serious split in the Python ranks.

There's little danger from Eric, who keeps himself very much to himself and will not get into costume unless he's absolutely certain that he will be seen.

I actually enjoy a fairly unrewarding afternoon as a revolutionary creeping up smoky passages – and have pleasant chats with Bernard (McKenna) and Andrew and others. We shoot till six in conditions of increasing discomfort.

Tuesday, September 26th, Monastir

Terry G is worried that TJ is driving everyone along at such a frenetic pace that he isn't leaving enough time to get the best shots. Gilliam is especially irked that the elaborately splendid detail of his marketplace is not being seen.

Thursday, September 28th, Monastir

Boring Prophet morning for me. Quite exhilarating as had to ad-lib most of the dull, droning speech. We did four or five takes and I tried to, or rather felt compelled to, make it a little different each time. Terry G spends most of the day coated in mud and does another of his extraordinary and grotesque gargoylical performances – this time as a Blood and Thunder Prophet.

Tonight at rushes (one-and-a-half hours' worth) my chief worry is the Ex-Leper. The dancing, prancing, gum-chewing character seems to go down well enough, but he looks like a cross between Tarzan and Geronimo – and somehow this detracts from the impact of the scene. As TJ says, he's the only character so far who has looked out of period. The Terrys agree, and a reshoot of this end part of the scene is scheduled for tomorrow.

Friday, September 29th, Monastir

A hard last day of the week. Into the small Ribat today, where a hypocaust has been constructed which is even harder to walk through than the tunnel. It's very hot, too, and besides being encumbered with extraordinarily clumsy props, there's an almost stifling smell of incense[1] inside the tunnels.

Redo the Ex-Leper ending. All sorts of things go wrong – a plane flies over, the Ribat lavatory attendant gets in shot. Terry G keeps strewing the ground where I'm standing for the Ex-Leper with scatterings of sheep's legs, squashed watermelons and foul-smelling water, around which the flies gather.

Then back to crouch in the tunnel again as Francis. John Stanier, the operator, says it isn't nearly as bad as filming forty feet down in a water-filled sewer in *Midnight Express.* It's now after seven and darkness has fallen on the Ribat. Comradeliness of night-shooting compensates for feeling of discomfort caused by dirt, very uncomfortable gear and cold wind.

Monday, October 2nd, Monastir

Wake at six. Today we're at Sousse, filming outside the city walls, where Zeffirelli filmed his crucifixion scenes.

The opening shot (of Mandy and Brian) seems to take forever, and I sit around, half-naked, made up as the Ex-Leper. An hour and a half before I'm used – leaping up, bronzed and fit, from a crowd of lepers at the city gates.

Tuesday, October 3rd, Monastir

A rather jolly day inside Matthias's room as plotting revolutionaries. Everyone on good form and much improvised joking. At lunchtime a meeting with John G and Anne H.

---

1. At this time, church incense smoke was regularly used by directors to create a diffused light. Later it was proved to be dangerous to health.

The subject of EMI's settlement came up. They are talking of offering us something by way of recompense but would probably insist on a secrecy clause. John C resisted this idea for a bit, but when told that the alternative was a possible two-year wait for a court hearing, he agreed quite sharply.

Wednesday, October 4th, Monastir

A long and arduous morning in Matthias's house. John Stanier is strapped into his Steadicam harness, which makes him look like a walking dentist's console.

John C takes Reg at a frenetic pitch, which loses all the nuances that had us rolling about in rehearsal. John becomes hot, tired and rather touchy as he tries to relax into the performance.

We slog on for three hours solid. There are no tea breaks as such out here, but Cristina and other unit ladies regularly do the rounds of crew and actors with water, Coca-Colas, coffees, etc., rather like the WVS or Meals on Wheels. By lunchtime it's finished, and John stays on to do the Centurion and Matthias in the afternoon.

Thursday, October 5th

Out to the location in Sousse. Clouds hamper progress today. On the slopes outside the impressive city walls, a huge, nude statue of me as Pilate is hauled towards the city on an oxen-drawn cart.

Spike Milligan turns up to do a part. He overplays thoroughly and becomes very testy when asked to wait for the clouds to pass for a retake. Mind you, I rather feel for anyone who arrives to help out and is asked to do a role which involves saying 'Let us pray' before being trampled by 300 Tunisian extras.

Sunday, October 8th, Monastir

The phone rings. It's JC. 'Have you got a couple of minutes, Mikey...?'

So I find myself spending the next hour or so rewriting the legendary, oft-written Scene 62 again.[1] Actually it turns out rather well,

---

1. In Mandy's kitchen, in which Judith tells the revolutionaries to stop talking and do something about it.

and we make each other laugh – and it is a lot better than what was there before.

Monday, October 9th, Monastir

A very gruelling day shooting the first Pilate scene. The need to keep the vital giggling ingredient fresh and spontaneous made it a little bit harder to play than an ordinary scene with set words and reactions. The success of this scene will depend on the genuineness of the guard's reaction to Pilate. It can't be all acted, it must be felt.

So I have to do a great deal of ad-libbing at the end of the scene – and by the end of the day I must have thought up over twenty new names for Biggus Dickus's wife – ranging from the appallingly facetious Incontinentia Buttox to the occasional piece of inspiration which resulted in breakdown from the guards. Bernard McKenna in particular did the nose trick spectacularly – once right down my toga.

Wednesday, October 11th, Monastir

The rushes include some good stuff at the gates of Sousse. But I find myself becoming very angry now whenever I see John wearing his tiny beard and moustache make-up – which was designed for him when he complained about the discomfort of full beards. So the rest of the crowd look wonderful – absolutely convincing biblical figures – and there, looming large on left of frame, is John looking like a sort of fourth-rate Turkish illusionist advertising on the back of *Stage*.

Friday, October 13th, Monastir

About 7.15 on this cold and unfriendly morning, the heavens open. The rain is relentless; there's no break in the clouds. The decision is taken to abandon [Ben's cell] for the day and to go into Matthias's house for our weather cover scene.

Change into Francis and drive myself up to the Ribat. It's a quarter to nine, the rain is heavier than ever, and the place is almost deserted. Rush into the nearest caravan, which happens to be Eric's. Eric and I watch the rain soaking the scaffolding and threadbare plaster walls of what remains of Zeffirelli's temple.

'This is filming,' Eric says, with a certain air of satisfaction.

At rushes this evening, I watch my endless takes of the first Pilate scene. Have never seen myself working so hard. Take after take – with instructions thrown out from behind the camera during the scene, making me seem like the dog at a sheepdog trial.

Monday, October 6th, Monastir

This time the weather looks more settled, and the Ben cell scene goes ahead. Aided by a bicycle saddle and two wooden pegs for my feet, I'm able to hang from real iron handcuffs, ten feet up a wall.

The first take sounds tight and unfunny. But the problem is that my movements are so restricted if my arms are *directly* above my head, that I'm mainly concerned with surviving rather than performing.

Anyway, the camera breaks down at this point, so we have pause for consideration. Decide to lower the manacles. This makes a tremendous difference and, though it's never very easy, I manage several takes full of the sarcastic vehemence that makes Ben funny.

Sunday, October 22nd, Monastir

Hotel Meridien, twenty to five in the afternoon. The suite is painfully quiet now Helen and the children have gone. Their presence had set a very different pace to this last week. On Saturday, Tom [aged ten] decided he would like to appear in the afternoon's filming, so he was supplied with a long robe and turban and looked very handsome. He was the only one of the Python children to have a go but was very proud of himself. The room was packed, and it was definitely one of the less comfortable scenes, but graced by the presence of the visiting George Harrison, who took the part of Mr Papadopolous, the impresario in charge of the Mount.

Sunday, October 29th, Hotel L'Oasis, Gabès

Friday's filming of the Sermon on the Mount [in Gabès] was difficult – mainly because we had a crowd of 600 local extras. Prouder, more independent, less malleable folk than up in Monastir.

Ken Colley performed marvellously as Jesus – using a modern translation of the Beatitudes, which we'd decided on in preference to the [King] James version, because it felt less like a set-up for a joke, and more of an attempt to portray Jesus as honestly as possible.

After the early takes, stunning in their recreation of the image of the Bible story, the extras started getting restless. At one point the crowd thought they were finished, and streamed from the Mount down towards the coaches, whilst Hammeda, one of our Tunisian assistants, pursued them screaming and shouting. The womenfolk had to be taken back early, because if they arrived back after sunset there would be hell to pay from the male villagers. All very different from the jolly, cooperative crowd who rolled on their backs at Monastir.

This morning I looked through an assembly of film – from Pilate's forum up to the crucifixions – and was greatly encouraged.

I'm not quite sure that I'd go along with TJ, who last night ventured to me that it was going to be 'a masterpiece', but having seen the stuff this morning, I feel closer to his judgement than to Terry Gilliam, with his analysis of shortcomings and missed opportunities.

Tuesday, October 31st, Gabès

Yesterday morning I was hauled up on the cross. It wasn't an unpleasant sensation, but I was stretched out for half an hour or so whilst various takes of Big Nose were done and, as I write, I've numbed a nerve in my left arm and lost some control of my muscles.

Thursday, November 2nd, Gabès

Today we spend most of our time and effort on the final song, which twenty-four crucifees sing as the climax of the film.

I'm in one of the front-row crosses. There's a slightly heady feeling – a tiny rush of vertigo as I clamber up onto the racing bicycle saddle (which protrudes absurdly anachronistically from an otherwise convincing cross). There's a certain sense of camaraderie amongst us all as we clip [on] our nails over the top of our hands and push aching arms through the ropes.

Among the few compensations is a wonderful view over the hills of Matmata.

Saturday, November 4th, Gabès

Sitting in one of the caravans waiting for us to be called, the talk turns to discussion of tomorrow's rest day. Roy Rodhouse, chief electrician, maintains this film has been a doddle – and anyone who's feeling the pressure ought to try 'a day or two with bloody David Lean – then they'll know what slave-driving is'.

Charles Knode [costume designer who assisted Hazel Pethig and played the Passer-By who utters the words, 'You jammy bastards!' after the flying saucer sequence] reckons it's been the hardest picture he's worked on – mainly because he feels his work isn't used. For instance, this week he's been up early to dress seventy-five extras each day, and the most they've eventually used is six of them.

There's no consensus of discontent, but from the attitudes of everyone I reckon the most disruptive element in any operation like this is lack of diplomacy – and that means regular attention to every department to make sure they're given time to air their grievances and lashings of appreciation.

Monday, November 6th, Gabès

Out to Matmata for the last time.

One long chasing shot has to be done all over again after one extra, wearing leather shoes, Terylene socks and smoking a cigarette, stops and looks straight into the lens, before being attacked with angry howls by Habib, Hammeda and the massed Anglo-Tunisian assistant directors.

Friday, November 10th, Carthage

Carthage is a comfy, bourgeois suburb – the Beverly Hills of Tunisia.

John dropped in for breakfast. We looked through Three Wise Men together. John Goldstone and Tim [Hampton] are of the opinion that we should aim to leave on Monday whatever happens – and that the amphitheatre close-ups and the Three Wise Men can be shot in London. The weather forecast offers no cause for hope.

At three we travel down to the location beside the sea, where amidst the bulky ruins of a Roman baths we are to shoot the Three Wise Men.

The roof of the stable drips occasionally as a welcome reminder that it *could* have been raining on Jesus's birthday. The costumes are excruciatingly hard to bear. My headdress is like having a sixty-pound haversack on one's skull, and both Graham and I have immense trouble with long, swirling trains – as we make an impressive exit, Graham's train catches on the door, rips down the middle and pulls the door off its hinges.

Saturday, November 11th, Carthage

At the amphitheatre at eight.

The consistent sunshine keeps us moving steadily forward, and my last shot of the movie is myself as one of the Revs 'flitting' through the streets. Then John, Eric and myself are finished.

A fine sunset – a great final curtain. Dinner at the Gulf restaurant with TJ, after rushes. He's pushed through thirty-six shots today and only the wide-shots of the amphitheatre, with Neil running away from the giant gladiator, remain to be done.

Editing and publicising *Life of Brian*;
a marketing trip to the US;
record album based on the film
soundtrack;
book of the film:
*Monty Python's Life of Brian /
Montypythonscrapbook*
(November 1978–August 1979)

1978–1979

Monday, November 20th

To the Hemdale Preview Theatre to see the assembly of all the *Brian* material. Apart from the Python team, Tim Hampton and John Goldstone, Anne Henshaw, George Harrison and Denis O'Brien were there. The whole preparatory assembly runs two hours and eight minutes.

General consensus is that it's a most encouraging viewing. Some scenes provoked gales of laughter – including the latter half of Ben and Pilate's audience chamber, the Hermit's hole, Brian's bedroom when the crowd arrive, and the Centurion and Matthias at the door of Matthias's house (the searching). There was a consistent level of interest and no embarrassments, though I confess to finding Otto dangerously like a cameo sketch.

The raid on Pilate's palace could be cut down too, by five or six minutes.

Wednesday, December 6th

At six o'clock I go down to John Goldstone's office in D'Arblay Street. He has a two-page ad for *Variety* to announce the completion of filming. It's odd, such a quiet man setting such store by making a noise, but I'm assured it's essential with million-dollar epics.

We both walk over to the Sapphire Theatre for the (much discussed and, for TJ, slightly feared) viewing of Julian Doyle's *Life of Brian*![1]

1. Julian [editor] had assembled an early working cut of the film, more or less on his own.

The film ran two hours and the reaction was very encouraging. The laughter (in scenes like Pilate's first audience chamber and the Gaolers in the cell) was long and loud. The song at the end worked and there was plenty of quite unequivocal applause.

Julian has done a good job and provided TJ with a well-shaped, well-structured cut on which he can work to tighten up all the details.

Tuesday, December 12th

Down to Neal's Yard. Hive of activity. Val Charlton[1] and Terry Gilliam are making Martians upstairs for the interior of the Flying Saucer in *Brian*, next door Terry J is editing and in the studio André has put together a demo of the new *Brian* song.

Wednesday, December 20th

I cheer myself up writing copy for J Goldstone's *Variety* ads for *Brian*.

Thursday, December 21st

Goldstone rings. He's very pleased with the *Variety* ad copy – it's going into early-Jan or mid-Jan issue. His plan is to create as much of a stir as possible inside the US before showing the assembly to distributors in late January. It's essential to arrange a US distribution deal at least six or seven months in advance in order to have any chance of booking up cinemas.

Saturday, January 13th, 1979

Terry J rang from a dubbing theatre at half past nine and, as in a call yesterday, referred to his paranoiac feeling of being 'ganged up' on by Julian and others at Neal's Yard during the editing. Terry G and Julian had sat together at the viewing and at a meeting afterwards Terry G had demolished all of the work Terry J had done.

Terry J must just be allowed to work as uninterruptedly as possible in order to make the film ready for the January 19th viewing.

1. Modelmaker and partner of Julian Doyle.

In a way, TJ's call was a cry for help and support, and I said I was prepared to go in and look at any edited film if it will help to get things ready any faster – but if it's merely to help TJ make a point, I said I felt that may be a waste of time at this stage.

Wednesday, January 17th

J Goldstone tells me that the Warner Brothers chief – John Calley – is very enthusiastic about the movie, thinks it could be one of the greatest comedies ever, but the only part they all seemed to find offensive was Graham's brief protestation, after his mother tells him he's the illegitimate son of a Roman, that he's a 'Hebe, a Kike, a Hooknose, a Yid, a Red Sea Pedestrian and proud of it!' Memorable words, written almost a year ago to the day by TJ and myself in Barbados, and now the only section of this deeply controversial film which offends every member of Warner Brothers' Board of Directors!

Friday, January 19th

Brian screening. Terry Hughes [producer/director on *Ripping Yarns*], Michael White, George H, Jill Foster. John Goldstone issues us with clipboards and little torches to make notes.

The showing does not go that well. Long periods of audience silence. But afterwards we all meet (Mafia-like) in a private room above the Trattoria Terrazza. General feelings are that the movie works 75%. Disagreement on cuts, however. TJ wants to lose stoning. Eric feels that the Ex-Leper should go before the stoning. All are agreed to cut Haggling and most of the raid. I suggest cutting Mandy's last speech. TJ agrees. Eric is worried about Otto – we all feel that it half-works.

Friday, February 2nd

At six I'm in De Lane Lea's basement for a preview of *Brian*.

The audience is three or four times the size of the last showing I attended, and, although the film is shorter, with Shepherds and a large part of the raid removed, I think it's the size of the audience that makes all the difference. They are much noisier in their appreciation and the end section goes particularly well.

I end up in The Carlisle Arms with Anne H, John G and Terry G and Julian. Julian is finding it almost impossible to spend any time on his own fine-cutting the movie without constant interruptions from Terry, over small points.

Saturday, February 3rd

I have to spend today at Neal's Yard, trying to patch up the wretched PR problems between editor and director. Gilliam arrives on his bicycle with a list of points on the film. Terry, Julian and myself sit and work amiably and constructively through the entire film, raising all the points from yesterday's viewing. Terry G's as well. TJ is amenable to most of the suggestions and some good cuts are agreed on.

Drive T back up to Hampstead at four. Terry acknowledges in one breath that Julian is an excellent editor, but at the same time bitterly accuses him of not taking a blind bit of notice of any of TJ's suggestions. I urge TJ to take a breather from the film – at least for twenty-four hours.

Tuesday, February 6th

Drive into Soho for one o'clock viewing of *Brian* – mainly for Eric who arrived back from LA last night. The showing is a good one and confirms my feeling after last Friday that the movie is consistently funnier than the *Grail*, but without the high points of visual and verbal felicity such as Trojan Rabbit and Black Knight fights.

[Despite warnings] that it will be X-rated because of the 'full-frontal' (what an absurd phrase anyway), it's a very funny scene, and Graham's reaction as he appears stark naked at the window, only to find 500 'followers' waiting to worship him, is one of the biggest and best laughs of the film.

Eric looks unhappy. He feels both Haggling and Ex-Leper should go. He is dissuaded from this, at least until they're dubbed – the general feeling being voiced by Julian, who claims that they are both scenes which people listen to and appreciate rather than roar with laughter at.

Clash over 'Brian of Nazareth' *Life of Brian* title suggestions. Eric says everyone in America he's talked to will be very disappointed if it's not 'Nazareth'. TJ and I maintain it's inviting a misleading comparison with *Jesus of Nazareth*.

Saturday, February 17th

Coffee at the Monmouth Coffee House, then across to the Bijou Theatre for another viewing of *Brian*. Sit next to Graham, who looks trim and healthy. Altogether a new, meek Graham. Then I remember he has got us here for a viewing no one particularly wants.

Afterwards, at a meeting at John Goldstone's office, Eric, Terry J, myself and Graham have a rather efficient, direct and radical appraisal of the movie. I now feel that the Ex-Leper sketch, funny though it ought to be, isn't getting the right reaction and is structurally holding up progress of the story at that early stage in the movie. Eric has always felt that and he feels Otto should go for the same reason. There is still a split on the title of the movie, however, between *Life of Brian* (John, Terry J and myself) and 'Brian of Nazareth' (the others).

Sunday, March 11th

Eric writes from the Chateau Marmont, thanking me for the *Life of Brian* book material and brimming over with facts and figures about the vast numbers of copies we'll be selling of this book we know nothing about. He's also floating the idea of an LA stage show in September.

Monday, March 12th

Graham Chapman rings from LA. Mainly to voice anxiety over a page of the book he has seen, which, he says, reads like the story of how Eric Idle put the *Life of Brian* together. We simply must see what is and isn't in it.

Sunday, March 18th, Black Horse Hotel, Skipton

Drive to the hotel in Skipton where I'll be staying for most of 'Golden Gordon' [an episode of *Ripping Yarns*].

Sunday, March 25th, Skipton

Retire to my low-ceilinged room looking out over the High Street to read through page proofs of the *Brian* book, which Eric has sent over. Vaguely unsettled by the balance/bias of the book.

Sunday, April 1st

Today we meet with Denis O'Brien. Eric brings the mock-up of the book, which looks wonderful and allays most of my fears. Everybody approves.

Denis O'Brien then fills us in on distribution information. Paramount, MGM, Twentieth Century Fox and Universal have all turned the film down. Paramount after being incredibly keen, until one powerful man on the board said no. Paramount and Universal both took offence at the unsympathetic Jews in the film (e.g. Otto, etc.).

Warner Brothers – or rather John Calley, one of their top men are keen, and Denis and George [Harrison] are happy to go with Calley although he is not offering them an enormous advance, or indeed any advance at all. But they like him. In passing Denis tells us that in fact there is more of his personal money at stake in this movie than George's – but then he smiles when we become solicitous and says, 'Well, if it bombs, it's just a couple of houses.' I must say he's the nicest rich man I know.

We talk about the stage show. Eric is like the Top Scholar of the Year at the Dale Carnegie School of Positive Thinking. A powerhouse of ideas, projects, facts – all very impressive.

He sees the stage show in LA as a glorious celebration of Python – and Denis comes in with fervent enthusiasm. It's all rather like a revivalist meeting. John C is most vocal in resisting the idea of an expensive, big theatre show. He wants to do it well in a smaller place. But I'm afraid Eric is right – we *could* fill the Hollywood Bowl.

Monday, April 2nd

Back to the Bijou Theatre for another viewing, with some of yesterday's adjustments made. A tiny audience, but I enjoyed the showing much better. 'Ben's Cell' scene is a strange phenomenon. It appears to be very delicately balanced at the opening. If it starts well, then there is great laughter all through, but if something goes wrong at the beginning (God knows why), it can go in silence.

Tuesday, April 3rd

Another Python session. This time to cover as much general ground as we can before Graham returns to Los Angeles tomorrow.

I get to 2 Park Square West by 6.30. They're just discussing the day's film viewing. 'Leper' is back in. It just hadn't worked without it. 'Otto' see-saws between condemnation and popularity. At the moment it's in favour. When discussion comes round to appropriately silly music to be played behind JC's dance, Graham suggests bagpipes, and I suggest the bagpipes play 'Hava Nagila'.

The meeting now rattles on with decisions coming thick and fast. I agree to supervise the making of the soundtrack album. JC will put together a short to go out with *Brian*.

One good and promising idea of [Eric's] is that Python set up its own label for the worldwide marketing of Python video cassettes – and also Python-related video cassettes, such as *Yarns*, *Rutland Weekend* and *Fawlty Towers*.

To round off the evening, Iain Johnstone brings his Python documentary (shot in Tunisia) to show us. It manages to make every one of us look articulate and quite amusing, but wittily avoids being pretentious itself or allowing us to be pretentious. An odd therapy to all sit round and hear ourselves saying things about each other on screen which we'd never say directly!

Monday, April 9th

Am up in my workroom by seven to look through the *Brian* book proofs and try to unblock some of the problem areas. Terry G is unhappy with the cover and wants me to try and bend Basil Pao's[1] ear on this, but TG is away in Cornwall, Cleese is in Jamaica, Eric seems to have washed his hands of the book now and is in Nice, and GC's in Los Angeles. So changes, if any, and improvements, are

---

1. Basil Pao, then working for Warner Bros in LA, designed the book. Now a writer and stills photographer, he has worked with me on six of my BBC travel shows and books.

down to what I can think up and work out with Basil between now and lunchtime.

Fortunately I'm feeling in quite a relaxed and creative mood and have written enough by the time Basil arrives at midday to satisfy me on several of the more problematical areas of the book. Basil, in turn, seems to be enjoying the book a little more now, after what sounds like an horrendous working experience in LA. I'm glad that Basil agrees with me on the changes – which will involve a week's more work, but which should still enable him to make the deadlines.

Wednesday, April 11th

At 7.30 down to Soho for a viewing of *Brian* (this must be around the twentieth public viewing). Terry J and I are the only Pythons. But, in a small audience, Barry Took (whom it's reassuring to see, considering his part in the birth of Python) and Yves de Goldschmidt, our natty, suave French distributor, who greets me very warmly with the news that *Grail* is still running in Paris.

'Otto' has been cut entirely from the movie for this showing. An enormous improvement. Tightens the impact of the film, without going off into extraneous areas.

Barry liked it, and Goldschmidt says afterwards that he reckons it a much more intelligent film than the *Grail*.

Thursday, April 12th

John Goldstone says the censor has been along to see *Brian* and reckons it would be an AA, and he liked it, but he is concerned about licensing a movie against which there could be legal proceedings. He is sure that the Festival of Light [a Christian Pressure group] will try and use the blasphemy law (upheld in the *Gay News* case) to try and stop the film. Lord Justice Scarman's judgement in the *Gay News* case[1] gives them a ridiculously wide area to play with. JG wants to be sure of the church's attitude, and so does the censor.

---

1. Scarman upheld the ruling under the Blasphemy Act of 1697 that the *Gay News* had offended by claiming that Christ was homosexual.

Sunday, April 22nd

TJ rings to ask me if I could spare time today to have another look at the 'Ben's Cell' scene. Although I bridle at the idea of endless re-editing, I think this is useful. There is something about 'Ben' which seems to hold it back from being as funny as it should and could be. We choose new takes of 'Ben', which improve the scene, I think.

Monday, April 23rd

J Goldstone tells me that EMI are re-releasing *Holy Grail* on a nationwide basis with *Blazing Saddles*. Fifty-fifty at the box office, and the whole double bill could be worth £400,000. So EMI are backing Python after all.

To help convince Warner Bros that they were doing the right thing in backing Brian, *Denis O'Brien corralled most of the Pythons into a marketing trip to Los Angeles.*

Saturday, June 2nd, Chateau Marmont, Los Angeles

Two limousines arrive to take us to the Bruin Theatre in Westwood where *Brian* is to be 'sneak previewed'. At the theatre we find a full house and 1,000 people turned away. Meet the Warners executives, who are, understandably, grinning pleasurably.

John Calley, our greatest supporter and second-in-command at Warners, turns out to be a very soft-spoken, pleasant-faced, tweed-jacketed forty-five to fifty-year-old, more like an English public-school headmaster than a Hollywood mogul.

It's a marvellous showing. Great laughs and applause on a scale we have not yet seen for *Brian*.

Sunday, June 3rd, Los Angeles

Out to Graham's long, low Brentwood residence. Denis O'Brien, benign as ever, arrives with some lunch – and can hardly contain his excitement over last night. Even he, who is one of the most level-headed men I've met, comes out with such assurances as 'You know, none of your careers will be the same after last night…'

Eventually we start the meeting and become a little more down to earth discussing what is still wrong with the movie. Warners are worried about the stretch from 'Leper' to 'Ben'. There is nothing but agreement for the 'Otto' cut.

We discuss our attitude to censorship, on which there is total agreement within the group that we do not and will not change anything because we're told to, unless we happen to agree that it isn't funny anyway. We're all happy to go to court in defence of the movie.

Monday, June 4th, Los Angeles

We drive out to Burbank Studios to talk to a small contingent (eight or nine) of Warner Bros marketing people.

Some of us, TJ especially, are concerned over the American fundamentalist Baptist backlash – after all, George Harrison, as producer, has already had letters threatening never to buy his records again – but Warners dismiss all this.

GC comes up with an excellent idea for Python movie no. 4 – 'Monty Python's World War II'. I think it could be a marvellous format for more of a sketch-type film – which everyone seems to want.

Thursday, June 14th

Another viewing of *Brian*. Small audience at the Bijou Theatre – all Pythons there, bar Graham. John Mortimer[1] and Oscar Beuselinck represent the law – Mortimer is to give us his opinion afterwards.

He's a nice, friendly, disarming man, with small, but not at all humourless, eyes, and a ready smile. He loves the film and reckons that we are quite safe. The chances of a jury convicting Python of blasphemy on the basis of this film are very remote, he believes – but not impossible. However, should an action be brought, Mortimer thinks it would take at least a year to come to court, by which time we'll have hopefully made our money and our point.

---

1. Barrister, playwright, novelist, creator of *Rumpole*.

Monday, June 25th

Drive out to Shepperton soon after eight to shoot a new opening to the much-filmed 'Ex-Leper' sequence – a last-ditch attempt to try and salvage a piece which everyone (with the possible exception of Eric) thinks ought to be in, but are not quite happy with. We shoot at the main gate of the old *Oliver!* set. The shooting, between showers and aeroplanes, goes along well, and we even do some hand-held dialogue shots.

Saturday, June 30th

Meeting at Denis's place in Cadogan Square. John C, Terry G and Terry J – the 'Home' Pythons – are all there. John G and Anne as well. Denis pitches in. He's never aggressive, never boorishly arrogant, but by God he's persistent. He would like to take on Python and any individuals in Python. He claims that his organisation (EuroAtlantic) will be able to minimise our UK tax liability on the money we earn from *Brian* – which could be substantial.

So, after very little hard talking, Denis has managed to persuade the four of us that we should let him 'structure' our earnings from *Brian* right away. I suppose this is the thin end of the wedge, and I expect that Denis and EuroAtlantic are with Python to stay.

Monday, July 2nd

Back into London for some dubbing and post-synching on *Brian*. The new work on the 'Leper' last week does seem to make the speech clearer, but I see-saw on the effectiveness of the sketch.

Thursday, July 5th

To John's for a writing session and discussion on film posters and publicity generally in preparation for the Warner launch. JC says he'll chair the meeting, as he's written a film on how to chair meetings – he means it half in fun, but mostly seriously.

Eric is in France and has sent a letter with suggestions. GC is in Los Angeles and has sent a request for another loan from Python. TJ bears gloomy news about our post-*Grail* tax situation. The authorities are getting tougher and could interpret our tax position in such a way that we fork out at least £60,000 of our *Grail* earnings to the government.

We spread out over his huge dining table (originally in Holloway prison) and churn out the sort of easy drivel which gives much pleasure and does not have to follow plot, story or character. JC works upstairs, writing heavily sardonic biographies of us all, and TG looks through photos.

I read out a long and inaccurate synopsis of the film which brought tears to assembled eyes (there is no better moment in one's creative life than hysterics at a first read!).

A new kind of summer holiday for the Palins this year. Instead of Europe, we stayed for almost a month at Al Levinson's house in the old whaling port of Sag Harbor on Long Island. [Al Levinson, writer and dramaturg for American Public Theater, became a friend in the late 1970s.]

Tuesday, July 31st, Sag Harbor

At about six – when my resources were not at their best after a long, hot, tiring day – the phone rang. It was Anne H, from London, ringing to say that Warners go to press on the posters in two hours.

They have finally rejected our unanimous Python ad-line 'He Wasn't the Messiah, He Was a Very Naughty Boy', and have suggested three alternatives – all of which are dreadful and tend to accentuate the 'outrageousness' of the movie.

Tuesday, August 14th

Terry Gilliam tells me that Eric was so unhappy with the Python soundtrack album André and I had produced, that he is working on a replacement. I feel not bitter, but just frustrated. I was never wholly keen on the live album. Eric was away and quite inaccessible for quick decisions and Warners wanted the album quick. So my work was wasted. I'm quite glad it at least stirred other Pythons into some sort of action.

Thursday, August 16th

I drive down in sunshine and scudding cloud to Neal's Yard.

Eric arrives heavily bearded. Graham is here too, and Terry G. We listen to the 'new' album – which is the stereo soundtrack *without* laughs, which evidently all the Pythons prefer. I must say the selection sounds lifeless, but Eric and Graham's ad-libbed links are funny.

At the end, all present okay the new album, but without enthusiasm. André does not look happy at the prospect of working for two more days – and probably nights – to complete this one. Eric and Graham will have to supervise the work. I refuse.

Life of Brian opens in the US,
then in the UK;
reactions
(August–November 1979)

1979

Friday, August 17th

Opening day for *Brian* in New York and Los Angeles. It seems difficult to grasp that we will actually be starting to get our money back, as from this evening. Terry J rang from New York. Canby's review in the *New York Times* was a rave, and the *Post* and *News* too were good.

Sunday, August 19th

A call from Denis on Fisher's Island to tell me that the audiences are rolling into *Brian*. Warners hoped for an $8,000 take at Cinema One on opening day and took $13,000. In Los Angeles all the movie houses showing *Brian* are good.

Wednesday, August 22nd

I have endeavoured, to help Anne and everyone else, to try and bring the five Pythons present in the UK together for a chat.

JC made the point that in the next Python film we should perhaps stick less to our rigid writing combinations and write with more fluidity. He thought this would help Eric, who always wrote by himself. 'I like writing by myself,' Eric countered, rather defensively.

I said I would rather not work on a new Python script for a full year. JC having proposed that we should all 'go somewhere very nice and just talk for two or three weeks about the subject'. I was called selfish by Eric. JC accused him of bullying. TG came in, as he said, to 'bail me out', by stating that he was not interested in working on another Python movie until he had completed something of his own. Graham said nothing.

But there is remarkable agreement thus far on the main points – that we should do another movie, that it should be completed within three to three-and-a-half years from now, and that World War II is a good area to start thinking in.

Friday, August 24th

T Gilliam arrives. He's in the middle of a debilitating hassle with Warners over the poster. They are determined to use their own wacky in-house ads that they first showed us in LA in June, and which we all immediately and instinctively disliked.

Saturday, September 1st

The copy of *Variety* I bought this morning has one entire page devoted to the condemnations of various religious groups. It looks as though we may become a major force for ecumenical harmony.

The next page shows that there are as many of open mind as there are of closed – we are the 21st top-grossing movie, despite playing at only three sites.

Wednesday, September 5th

George Harrison calls. He went to see *Brian* – found a one-third black audience and a row of Orthodox Jews – all enjoying it.

But he does tell me of an exquisite piece of justice. Whom should George find himself in the first-class lounge at Kennedy with, but Bernard Delfont – the man who turned down *Life of Brian*. George was not backward in going forward and in an informal way enquired whether or not Bernie was acquainted with the fact that Python had taken £1 million already. George thanked him profusely.

Wednesday, September 12th, Plaza Hotel, New York

Denis O'B, eyes sparkling like a child with a new toy, buttonholes each of us with the good news that 600 cinemas throughout the US will be taking *Brian* by early October and, because of the performance and reputation of the movie so far, Warners have been able to do deals split 90/10 with the exhibitors (90 to Warners, 10 to the exhibitors). The *Grail's* deals were 50/50 usually.

Thursday, September 13th, New York

At twelve I stand in for Eric in an interview for the *Washington Post* book column. We chat for a half-hour, but I take a while to settle, having been far more rattled than I should have been by EI's outburst over our Tom Snyder *Tomorrow* show interview. Eric, who has become far more obsessed with the interviews than I would have expected from such a press-hater, berates me for mentioning the *Gay News* blasphemy case and the Jorgen Therson *Sex Life of Christ* in the same breath as *Brian.*

The Snyder interview was not just about *Brian* – that got good plugs – it was also about censorship, and that's why I instanced the two cases. It's a one-o'clock-in-the-morning show, it was a relief to be able to talk about our concerns in some detail – and it now turns out that Eric is in favour of censorship – at least in interviews, which I can't accept.

At Terry Gilliam's apartment, with fine views of the New York canyons below, a party develops. Eric is by now utterly mellow and a quite changed man. He apologises for this morning's episode and says he has since rung a friend in LA, who thought the *Tomorrow* interview was very good.

Monday, September 17th, White Caps, Fisher's Island

Denis had softened us up the night before, when we had a premeeting meeting to discuss agendas, etc., so it was no surprise to us when he began his pitch this morning by strongly advising a sooner-rather-than-later schedule on the new movie, the argument being that he would like to strike while *Brian* is hot.

Warners want a deal, and Paramount too. Denis reckons at the moment he can, with a few trimmings, go to Warners and get a percentage-of-gross deal. Something like 10 or 15% of gross – which means 10 or 15 cents of every dollar paid at the box office. (Usually this would be a percentage of distributor's gross.) He would like to try and prise *Grail* away from Cinema 5 and give it to Warners together with our German film as a double-bill potboiler for next summer.

Enthused by Denis's evangelical approach, and in good spirits because of *Brian*'s success here, there is little opposition to a tighter schedule to the new movie than that discussed in mid-August. In fact, by the end of the morning session, we have agreed to a delivery date for the finished movie in November 1981. Shooting would be in March/April 1981.

Tuesday, September 18th, Fisher's Island

After breakfast we begin our first group session on the fourth film. I think JC brings up the same sequence that he did when we first began *Brian*. In which a spacecraft with alien beings looking just like us lands. The beings emerge, give a stirring message of hope to the world, turn to re-enter their ship and find they've locked themselves out.

Other suggestions are a sci-fi movie of a vision of the future where everything's almost exactly the same. Or a state of war – but a war which is always in the background. Or a vision of Hell, or Monty Python's 'Utopia'.

Denis, walking by the pool, looks anxiously at us for signs of A Great Breakthrough or A Hugely Commercial Idea, or at the very least some outward and visible sign that genius has been at work.

In a scenario which is more like what one reads in the back of *Private Eye*, Denis tells us of the bizarre odyssey that some of our earnings will make, via Holland, Panama and Switzerland.

Not that Denis is sensational as he tells us of this wonderland of vastly increased wealth. But occasionally John and I have to laugh when he strays into the satirisable. When we re-emerge into the dwindling sunlight around the pool at 5.30 this afternoon, we have all become accomplices in something most of us don't understand.

Sunday, September 23rd

Terry G comes round in the evening and gives me the first 'unofficial' inkling of *Brian*'s progress in the States. Apparently one-and-a-half million dollars were taken in the first couple of days (Thursday/Friday) and Warners are now looking beyond a $25 million gross.

TG is caught. He has stated that he will and must do his own movie in the next two years. He only wants to do animation and a bit of performing for Python. Can he do both and resist Eric's suggestion that he alone should direct Python 4?

Wednesday, September 26th

To Methuen for a preliminary meeting on the launch of *Monty Python's Scrap Book* on November 15th. So good to be amongst publishers who actually sell books. They've stood by us well.

Thursday, September 27th

Talk to Denis O'B after breakfast. He says he's almost 'too embarrassed' to talk about *Brian* figures, but on the first three days of our 'break' in the US (this is film-man's jargon for first nationwide exposure), we have broken nine house records and done 250% better business than Warners next best this summer – *The In-Laws*. He confirms the figure of one-and-a-half million dollars taken in the first three days in 120 cinemas.

Friday, September 28th

Visit EuroAtlantic in mid-afternoon. Denis feels bound to ask me why Terry G, after proving his directorial ability so clearly in *Jabberwocky*, didn't get to handle *Life of Brian*. So I try to fill him in on a little Python folklore.

From Denis's I drive to Shepherd's Bush to John Jarvis's cutting rooms, where JC is on the final stages of preparation of the Pythonised travelogue[1] which will make up the complete all-Python bill when the *Life of Brian* opens in London.

John is in his element with the slowly building rant, which he can take to hysteria and beyond like no one else I know. Suggest a couple of cuts which he seems happy with.

---

1. It was a traditional, bland piece about Venice, made special by John's commentary – 'gondolas, everywhere fucking gondolas'.

Wednesday, October 3rd

Python's *Life of Brian* has made No. 1 on the latest *Variety* chart. One year to the day since we were packed in a tiny upper room of the Ribat in Monastir, ours is the film most people in America want to see.

Tuesday, October 23rd

Last night TG saw Denis, freshly returned from LA, but found him strangely low. None of the deals he'd gone to the States to make had been made – the main reason being a 30-35% dive in *Brian* business on the very weekend Denis arrived in the US.

I gather we are now banned in South Carolina – the first *state* to prohibit *Brian* – thanks to the activities of that great fighter for human rights, Governor Strom Thurmond.

So the backlash has finally hit, and Denis is now trimming his estimates about the gross. He now seems happy to settle for a total of 24 or 25 mill, across the US, which would leave a distributor's gross of 15 mill. Still way above anything the *Grail* did, but nevertheless bigotry, prejudice and intolerance – or pure and untarnished ideals – have at last shown there is a limit to *Brian*'s heady progress.

Friday, October 26th

Anne H has asked to have a meeting with me. She doesn't look cheerful and what she has to say is disturbing. Her 'relationship' with Denis has crumbled to nothing. After various attempts to acquire information (on our behalf) about matters such as copyright of Python material – songs, etc. – Denis became very sharp with her and they haven't spoken for two weeks.

I had fears that this transition would not be easy, but I am a little worried by the uncompromising toughness that Denis is showing to those who are our friends and those whose value and service to us is proven – Anne and André, to name but two.

Monday, October 29th

A party at the ICA and a showing of *Brian* for the crew. About 300 people there – all the old faces of those who were either hoisting me up on crosses, or making the crosses, or filming me being hoisted up, one year ago today.

Thursday, November 1st

A large Jaguar picks me up after lunch and takes me down to a BBC interview at Broadcasting House, this time with Gerald Priestland for the networked *Today* programme. John C is also on with me.

Priestland is enormous – he's actually *taller* than John, but amiable and donnish. They play back his review of the film, which swings from great praise – 'very funny… Pythons at their best' – to a note of distinct criticism for our handling of the 'Crucifixion' sequences – or for the 'Crucifixion' sequence period. He equates it with 'whistling at Auschwitz' and to him it appears that we are condoning suffering.

JC answers smoothly, as if he's rehearsed. I become a little tongue-tied faced with Priestland's penetrating stare and huge bulk. But the interview seems to pass off well. Priestland is not huffy or offended.

Wednesday, November 7th

My mother really does fear public outcry, picketings and general national anger. I was able to tell her that the Festival of Light are now taking a much saner view of the movie and come to the conclusion that 'it is extremely unlikely that the film would sustain a successful prosecution in English law'.

Friday, November 9th

I go for a run across the Heath. Tonight is our confrontation with Muggeridge and the Bishop of Southwark (on BBC's *Friday Night, Saturday Morning*) and, as I squelch through the now-leafless beechwoods and around West Meadow, with Kenwood House a glittering white symbol of order and reason in the background, I sort out my thoughts about *Brian*, and the points that the movie tried to make seem to be all to do with power – its use and abuse by an establishment.

As I work in the afternoon on committing to paper some of my morning's thoughts, I find myself just about to close on the knotty question of whether or not I believe in God. In fact, I am about to type 'I do not believe in God', when the sky goes black as ink, there is a thunderclap and a huge crash of thunder and a downpour of epic proportions. I never do complete the sentence.

Over drinks we meet Tim Rice, the presenter – tall, open, unassuming and quite obviously a sensible and sympathetic fellow – then little gnomic Muggeridge – great smile and sparkling eyes – and Mervyn Stockwood, the Bishop of Southwark – big, impressive, avuncular, cradling the second of his whiskies and complaining gently that he'd been told the wrong time of the film and had missed 'some of it'. But his chaplain had told him all about it, he assured me.

JC was, and always is, nervous at first and had asked Tim Rice to direct his early questions at me! This was quite an easy task, and I felt that I was being as fluent and as relaxed as I'd ever been. We must have talked for ten to fifteen minutes, getting a few laughs, making very clearly the point about Brian not being Jesus and the film not being about Jesus, and I think keeping the audience amused.

Then Stockwood and Muggeridge joined us and were asked for their opinion of the film. From the moment that Stockwood, resplendent in his purple bishop's cassock, handsome grey hair, fingering his spectacles and his cross with great dexterity, began to speak, I realised his tack. He began, with notes carefully hidden in his crotch, tucked down well out of camera range, to give a short sermon, addressed not to John or myself but to the audience.

In the first three or four minutes he had brought in Ceauçcscu and Mao Tse-tung and not begun to make one point about the film. Then he began to turn to the movie. He accused us of making a mockery of the work of Mother Teresa (a recent Nobel Prize winner), of being undergraduate and mentally unstable.

He made these remarks with all the smug and patronising paraphernalia of the gallery-player, who believes that the audience will see he is right, because he is a bishop and we're not.

'If there'd been no Jesus, this film would not have been made,' crowed Stockwood. I wanted to say, 'If there had been no Jesus, we wouldn't have needed to make the film.'

Muggeridge, in his odd, obsessive way, accused us of denigrating the one man responsible for all the [finest] works of art ever made and other thoroughly irresponsible digs. Vainly did John try and remind him that there were *other* religions in the world, that there *was* a civilisation before Jesus, that there have been artists who have *not* painted the Crucifixion or written about the Incarnation, and the world's religions have never been above a bit of torture if it suited them.

No, Malcolm was gone, set on a bizarre course, armed with his own navigational guides, and nothing we could do could prevent him going straight for the rocks. But the Bishop was meanwhile throwing himself off the cliffs. Outrageously dismissing any points we made as 'rubbish' or 'unworthy of an educated man', he posed and preened and pontificated. And he ended the long 'discussion' by saying he hoped we would get our thirty pieces of silver.

In the hospitality room we were surrounded like heroes returning from a war. I was introduced to Raymond Johnston of the Festival of Light – always our most arch-enemies.[1] Instead I found myself confronted with a thin, rather nervous man, a committed Christian, who had been embarrassed at the display of the Bishop. He (Johnston) *had* seen the film. He had found it quite clear that Brian and Jesus were separate people. He had many differences of opinion with us, but he thought the film not malicious, not harmful and, furthermore, he saw and appreciated that we were making very valid points about the organised religions which told you what to think, in the same way that Stockwood tonight had used the cheapest and most dishonest methods to tell people what to think.

Later I watched it go out and fortunately the Bishop's 'performance' came over as badly on air as it did in the studio. TG rang as the last words of the interview faded and ranted with anger for a full half-hour. He thought that the programme was Python's finest hour since the ABC trial.

Sunday November 11th

The Sunday reviews – the last main batch, thank God – are very favourable. *The Observer* is a rave, as are most of the popular papers (from whom I expected more disapproval). Once again the *Telegraph*

---

1. They had called for the film to be banned. 'Though not in itself blasphemous, it will tend to discredit the New Testament story of Jesus in confused semi-pagan minds.'

shrinks from enthusiasm – as if unwilling to endorse us, which I regard as a sign that we may have hit the Establishment quite hard on the nose. But they positively state that the film will not harm anyone, and there should be no 'shades of the Ayatollah' over *Brian*.

Wednesday, November 14th

Letter in the *Guardian* from the Vicar of Hampstead, very critical of Stockwood and Muggeridge, thinks that the Church needs its pretensions pricking by such as Cleese and myself.

Denis O'B rings to say that the first-week take at the Plaza is £40,000. 'Forty thousand pounds!' Denis incredulates in tones of almost religious fervency. It is impressive and has beaten the previous highest-ever take at the Plaza (which was for *Jaws*) by £8,000, with seven fewer performances. So all the publicity has had maximum effect.

Writing the new film:
The Meaning of Life;
new record album:
Monty Python's Contractual Obligation Album
(November 1979–July 1980)

1979–1980

Monday, November 19th

Started work on the new Python movie.

JC thinks war is a limiting subject. EI and myself both see it in wider terms. The talk then shifts, or is shifted by TJ who is lobbying indefatigably for World War III, to a science-fiction world of the future. Where very little has changed. Possibly a benevolent and very well-meaning society in which everything is attended to, but it is quite unworkable. Enormous queues to complain everywhere. Everyone born into this society, I suggest, is handed a raffle ticket on birth which gives him or her the chance of being PM eventually.

Some good chat – generally concerned with revealing the idiocy of many of our rules and regulations, hardly a new area, but there is a certain satisfaction in the combined strength of all our input.

We walk in the park, then lunch at our 'regular' round table by the window at Odin's. We become very happy, and it's decided that we shall not shackle ourselves with too much discussion – we shall go away for a couple of days and write *any*thing. We pledge ourselves, like the Three Musketeers, that we will do all in our power to bring about a silly film. JC warns, splendidly, that 'We'll show them how silly a film can be.'

Thursday, November 22nd

TJ has written a classic piece about soldiers presenting their officer with a clock under fire. Really funny. We complete that and by 5.45 find ourselves with a large output – maybe twenty or twenty-five or 25 minutes, for the meeting tomorrow.

Friday, November 23rd

A very angry, abusive letter to *The Times* from a man called Allott in Finchley, who clearly doesn't like the *Life of Brian*, but admits he hasn't seen it. It is proposed to send a Python reply to *The Times* saying 'We haven't seen Mr Allott, but we don't like him.'

Finally we start to read the first sketches of the new movie. Eric has a couple of quite tart monologues, then I read the first of our two blockbusters. It's received with much nodding and the '*Some* good bits' line. JC reads a long and rambling and not awfully funny piece about Kashmir and sex and male brothels, which doesn't go down very well. It's our second effort (mainly TJ's), including the clock presentation, which is the one big hit of the session.

Monday, December 3rd

JC and GC, some very funny material (at last) of the British Raj sort. Gilliam has a wonderful idea for a cartoon in which the town fights the countryside – and one marvellous idea of Central Park in NYC spilling its banks and flooding the city with green.

All in all we have about thirty minutes of a very good TV show to show for our two weeks on the film. But morale is high – we seem to be getting on together well.

Thursday, December 6th

Decide to call in [on Robert Hewison] at Stanton St John.

We talk over his proposal to write an official Python biography, which was turned down by the chaps – for the moment anyway. I don't think people could face any more interviews about the past. But I will press for Robert to be made chronicler of the *Brian* struggle. I think there is a useful book to be done on the whole controversy and its various manifestations.[1]

---

1. This was eventually commissioned by Geoffrey Strachan at Methuen and came out as *Monty Python: The Case Against* in 1981. It is the first, best and last word on the history of Python's run-ins with the censor.

Friday, December 14th

I committed a rather rushed song called 'I Was Born Sir Keith Joseph's Double' to tape as my only contribution to this afternoon's 'Python Sings' record meeting.

Round to E. Idle's in Carlton Hill at 2.30. Terry J had written ten songs or fragments of songs. All rather sweet – sung into his pocket tape recorder in Terry's delightfully doleful voice, which wanders occasionally into areas of deep tunelessness.

Sunday, December 23rd

Brian is top film in London yet again and the *Life of Brian* book is up to No. 3.

Sunday, December 30th

The 1980s will be interesting. Python has established itself and we are now in an almost unassailable position of respect and comfortable living – and we now have to face up to the prospect of what the hell we do with this respect, freedom and comfort. They're not always the bedfellows of creativity.

Wednesday, January 9th, 1980

At Redwood (Studios) [Neal's Yard] at four. Eric, moderately well laid-back, occasionally strumming guitar. Trevor Jones[1] bustling. André looking tired, but working faithfully. Graham, who is getting £5,000 a month from Python as co-producer of this album (*Monty Python's Contractual Obligation*), sits contentedly. He seems, as usual, not quite in tune with what's going on around him. I record the Headmaster's speech and that's about all.

---

1. Trevor Jones, composer. To avoid confusion with the film composer of the same name he is now known as John Du Prez. Wrote the music for a number of Python songs as well as for the film *A Fish Called Wanda* and, with Eric Idle, the musical *Spamalot*.

Friday, January 11th

To Denis O'B for a meeting at two. For the first time we are being offered the prospect of quite considerable financial rewards. At the moment he seems to have admirable goals, but I have this nagging feeling that our 'freedom' to do whatever we want may be threatened if Denis is able to build up this juggernaut of Python earning power and influence. A few of the most interesting projects may be rolled flat.

Monday, January 14th

To Anne's for a Python meeting with Denis to discuss Denis's two offers for the next (Monty Python) movie – from Warners and Paramount. Warners want a screenplay before going ahead, Paramount just a treatment. Denis is asking for 6.4 million dollars.

Time is of the essence, as Paramount, who are offering a better financial deal, do require the movie for summer 1981 release. This, I feel, puts pressures on the group which we would rather not have – and thankfully no one feels any different. But JC suggests that we go along with Paramount at the moment and just see if, after the seven-week March/April writing period, we have enough to give them a treatment – 'In which case we could all go ahead and make a lot of money very quickly.'

Though we all feel the Paramount deal for the next movie is the one to pursue, Denis is proposing to try and place *Grail*, now released from Cinema 5, with Warners, so they can do a *Life of Brian/Holy Grail* re-release in the US next summer. There is no great enthusiasm for selling the Bavaria film as a Python Olympic Special to the US networks in summer of this year.

André arrives very late, bringing a quite beautiful tape of Trevor Jones's arrangement for 'Decomposing Composers'. How the hell I'll sing it, I don't know.

Monday, February 18th

Down to Redwood Studios, where Eric, TJ and myself record 'Shopping Sketch' and 'All Things Dull and Ugly', plus one or two other snippets for the album.

From Redwood round to Anne's to take in some more Python scripts from last autumn's writing session to be typed up in preparation for Wednesday's meeting. What is rapidly becoming apparent about *Brian* is that Denis's forecast of earnings from it in 1980 was drastically over-optimistic. The £250,000 figure he mentioned in November now looks likely to be nearer £40,000.

Although the distributor's gross in the US was over nine million dollars, over four million was spent on publicity and advertising – and this was where Warners were weakest. Their posters and their slogans were constantly changed, and we never approved any of them – now they present a bill for this fiasco which is equal to the entire production budget of the film.

The upshot is that not only will there be not a penny profit from America from a movie which was one of the top-forty grossers of the year in the US, but the earnings will hardly cover half the production cost. So the chance of making any more money – beyond our £72,000 fee for writing and acting – depends on the rest of the world. Fortunately the UK is looking very strong, Australia is holding up well and France and Germany remain to be seen.

Wednesday, February 20th

Pick up Eric on the way to JC's. Everyone there and chortling over the latest and looniest batch of selected press cuttings about *Brian*. It's noted that Swansea has banned the film totally. Four hundred people in Watford are petitioning because the local council have recommended the film be an 'X'.

Coffees are poured and we settle round JC's ex-prison table, which now seems to be Python's favourite writing venue. No one wants to spend time on business, we all want to write and make each other laugh, but business has to be done, so it's decided that we will make a clean sweep of it today. So Anne stays with us, and Denis is summoned at three.

The disillusion with Hollywood and all things to do with Warners and *Brian* lead us into thinking how nice it would be to do a small-budget film just for the fun of it – keeping our own control and making money in the way *Grail,* with its modest budget, did, and *Brian*, with its Hollywood campaign, didn't. Denis is anxious to set up all sorts of production and syndication deals in the US, and he's talked to CBS about two Python TV specials, for which we would be paid $700,000 each.

No one wants to do specials for the US, but there is still the German material. Suddenly it all gels. We will use the German material, plus some old sketches, plus anything we wrote in October/November and reshoot as a quick cheap movie. The mood of the group is unanimous. Fuck Hollywood. Fuck CBS. Let's do something we enjoy in the way we want to do it – and so economically that no one gets their fingers burned if a Hollywood major *does* turn it down.

D O'B seems unable to respond at our level and talks business jargon for a while. I like Denis, and I think he likes us, but he is only in the early stages of finding out what everyone who's ever dealt with Python has eventually found out – that there is no logic or consistency or even realism behind much of our behaviour. No patterns can be imposed on the group from outside. Or at least they can, but they never stick; they crack up, and the internal resolutions of Python are the only ones that last.

Monday, February 25th

Eric and John have searched the archives, Terry J has been away, GC doesn't appear to have done much, but I saved my bacon by writing an extension to 'Penis Apology',[1] which produced an outstandingly good reaction. Near hysteria. I think Python is definitely working out all the repressions of childhood – and loving it!

Tuesday, February 26th

Round to Eric's. That's very cheering – mainly because all of us are happy to be together at the moment, and the tapes that André's prepared of the sketches and songs for the LP assembled by Eric, with a certain amount of gentle bullying over the last two months, are a great boost.

---

1. 'Penis Apology' was a very long-drawn-out health advisory at the beginning of the film warning the audience that there may be a penis in shot later on. The apology became longer and more complex, including discussions from bishops for the Church's view, etc. It was never used.

Friday, February 29th

TJ has written something which he cheerfully acknowledges as the ultimate in bad taste – it's all about people throwing up – very childish, but rather well controlled, dare I say – it had me in as prolonged and hysterical a bout of laughter as I can remember.

Thursday, March 6th

To Eric's for a Python readthrough. Eric is being very friendly, warm and accommodating. Terry Gilliam isn't there (which provokes some rumblings of discontent from Eric, who, I think, being unaligned to either of the main writing groups, feels that TG's absence deprives him of an ally). GC is as avuncular and benign as ever.

JC reads out an outrageously funny schoolmaster sex-demonstration sketch. Our stuff doesn't go quite as well as expected this morning. Eric has a chilling ending for the film, when the outbreak of nuclear war is announced. He's been reading about the dangers of, and plans in the event of, nuclear war happening.

Wednesday, March 12th

Over lunch we discuss the general balance of material, which seems to fall into School, War/Army and North-West Frontier. Lists are made in the p.m. and a putative running order worked out. This is the stage when there is much talk of 'What is the film about?' and how we can relate the various themes – whether we should start conventionally or with an apology for what's to be seen. Quite good progress.

Wednesday, March 26th

Leave for the airport at a quarter past three for the Python promotion in Paris. *Python Sacré Graal* is in its 71st week of its third reissue in Paris! So clearly there is a cult here, and it's based on only one movie.

Thursday, April 3rd

Some progress, but nothing sweeps the gathering off its feet. JC reaches a peak of frustration. 'Nine weeks of writing,' he practically sobs in anguish, 'and we haven't got a *film.*'

But we make lists and from the best elements – mainly 'Kashmir' – I suggest that we play six members of a family – a sort of Python saga, set in the *Ripping Yarns* period of 1900-1930. The idea of telling the story of a family seems to appeal and quite suddenly unblocks the sticky cul-de-sac we appeared to have written ourselves into. It suits me, a *Yarns* film with all the team in it – something I've often been attracted to.

So, quite unexpectedly, the day turns around. At the eleventh hour we have a style, a subject and a framework for the new film.

Tuesday, April 8th

Drive over to Eric's for a Python meeting about the next album, which we have to deliver under the terms of our Arista/Charisma contract.

Eric suggests we call the album 'Monty Python's Legal Obligation Album' and I suggest that we have it introduced by some legal man explaining why we have to deliver it and the penalties if we don't. This replaces the tentative 'Scratch and Sniff' title.

Monday, April 28th

At Park Square West to meet Ron Devillier, who is on his way back to the US after a TV sales fair in France. Ron is anxious to market the Python TV shows in the US and, in view of his pioneering work in awakening the US to [*Monty Python's Flying Circus*], we listen to him with interest.

Cleese, who had not met Ron before, clearly warmed to him, and at the end of an hour's discussion (Ron emphasising the extraordinary audience ratings which Python still picks up whenever it's shown in the US), John proposed that we should meet in a week's time, when all of us reassemble for the recording of *Python's Contractual Obligation Album*, and we should agree to approach Ron formally and ask him to set out his terms for distributing Python tapes.

Denis is quite actively pursuing a company called Telepictures Inc., who he hopes can be persuaded to handle *all* Python product (in and out of the series).

Again the big-business approach of Denis confronts and seems to conflict with the decentralised Python plans, which are born of mistrust of big American companies and trust in individuals whom we like instead. I foresee the Telepictures v Ron Devillier situation becoming a head-on battle between Denis's 'philosophy' and our own.

Tuesday, June 3rd

Listen to the Python *Contractual Obligation Album*. I'm afraid it does sound rather ordinary. One or two of the songs stand out and there are some conventional sketches of Cleese and Chapman's ('Man Enters Shop', etc.) which are saved by good performances. 25% padding, 50% quite acceptable, 25% good new Python.

Wednesday, July 2nd

We talk briefly about Python's general biz. Denis's call for a business meeting and a meeting to discuss his exciting new proposals for a distribution network of our own are met with almost universal lack of interest. 'Tell him we went off to sleep,' John advises Anne when she is desperately asking what reaction she should relay to D O'B about his proposals.

JC wants a month of leisurely talk and discussion and does not want to face the 'slog' of nine-to-five writing. I suggest that we don't yet have a very clear and positive area or identity for the subject matter of the film and that we should only write when we are really 'hungry' to write. But it's Graham who quite blandly drops the real bombshell – he's working for the next few days on a *Yellowbeard* rewrite and then he hopes to film it in Australia during the winter [Graham Chapman's film, featuring Eric Idle, Marty Feldman and Nigel Planer, with a cameo from John Cleese, was released in 1983.] This straight pinch from previously discussed Python plans is a real stunner and the well-controlled indignation of Eric and Terry J rises to the surface.

I have the increasing feeling that we are going through a period similar to the post-*Grail* days in '75, '76, when individual Pythons want to stretch their legs. Terry G led the field with *Time Bandits*, I've done the *Yarns* and the 'Railway' documentary.

This lunch and the discussions were all part of the painful process of preserving Python. We don't fit into any easy patterns, we ask each other to make enormous compromises, adjustments and U-turns, but we do produce the best comedy in the country.

Monday, July 14th

Hurry through the rain to 2 Park Square West and a Python meeting.

All Pythons present except Gilliam. Denis has greatly looked forward to this meeting, for this is the first time he has aired his latest proposal to the group as a whole. The proposal is that Python should become involved in the setting-up of an independent UK film distribution company – HandMade Films.

Denis rides all interruptions as he slowly and impressively reveals his plans. But he is not a good judge of people – and of English people especially – and instead of being received with wide-eyed gratitude, his proposals are subjected to a barrage of strong scepticism.

Eric wants to know how much it all will cost us and then queries whether or not we need it, as it will mean yet another source of interminable business meetings. John C queries Denis's assumption that there will be eight 'Python-based' films at least in the next five years. He certainly isn't going to do one, and neither is Eric. Also the assumption that *Time Bandits* and *Yellowbeard* will each make at least £650,000 in the UK is received without conviction.

Denis's worst enemy is his own ingenuous enthusiasm in the face of five very complex, quite sophisticated minds, four at least of which distrust one thing more than anything else – uncritical enthusiasm. So it's left undecided.

Denis rather rapidly runs through the rest of the agenda, but he's lost us. The more he enthuses over terms, deals, percentages, controls, etc., the more John turns his mind to doing anagrams on his agenda (he had a good one for Michael Palin – i.e. Phallic Man).

To lunch at Odin's. Terry suggests the group should spend three days in Cherbourg, writing. John thinks we should do a film about the Iliad. Denis looks bewildered.

Monty Python at the Hollywood Bowl:
live show, record album and short film;
work continues on writing
The Meaning of Life
(July 1980–July 1981)

1980–1981

Monday, July 21st

Anne rings early to say that Python has been offered four days at the Hollywood Bowl at the end of September. Two weeks in LA in late September, all together, would, I feel, do our writing chances and the group's general commitment to working together so much good that we should decide to go ahead with it as soon as possible.

Wednesday, July 23rd

TJ comes up after lunch. Complete 'Sperm Song'.

In the evening I ring John C to find him very disappointed with his writing progress. He claims not to have been really well since last Friday and says that he and GC have not written much and he doesn't like the family idea and could we not postpone the entire film for six months?

Friday, July 25th

JC proposes a moratorium on the film – period unspecified. This rather deflating proposal is perhaps made more acceptable by a general welcoming of the Hollywood Bowl show. We shall be together for two or three weeks in LA in late September, we will do four nights at the Bowl, and it is agreed that it shall be videotaped for sale to US TV.

No one has yet really decided how long this 'interruption' should be. Six months is the minimum. But six months merely means an almost impossibly short period for the resolution of any alternative plans, so a year is proposed. And reluctantly accepted. We shall meet again to write the movie in September 1981.

Thursday, July 31st

To EuroAtlantic for what is supposed to be a couple of hours of business and a couple of hours of thought on the content of the stage show. It turns out to be four hours of business and hardly a thought for the content.

Once again Denis pushes us towards the Telepictures video deal and the distribution company. All of us weaken on Telepictures, apart from Eric, who maintains that we should not give video rights for seven years to a company we know nothing about and vetoes the agreement until he's thought about it more.

Thursday, August 21st, Copenhagen and Malmö

To Copenhagen (for *Life of Brian* publicity) with Terry J and Anne Bennett (of CIC, our distributors). From this neat, clean, modest little capital we took a neat, clean hydrofoil across to Malmö in Sweden.

I hear from TJ (confirmed by Anne Bennett) that Python has not begun too well in Germany. Strong religious anti-reaction in Stuttgart – elsewhere sluggish. So Brianity is perhaps not to be the new world religion after all.

Friday, August 22nd, Copenhagen

At about ten o'clock we start interviews in our room, followed by a press conference downstairs, after which we are to give a TV interview. The Danes and Swedes both find the Norwegians a Scandinavian joke – slow-witted, thick-headed, humourless fishing folk – and they send them up unmercifully. The fact that Python's *Life of Brian* has been banned in Norway causes our hosts great glee and the Swedes have a poster tagging the film 'So Funny it was Banned in Norway'.

Saturday morning, September 20th, Los Angeles

[To] our rehearsal room for a first look at the script [of our Holly-wood Bowl show]. In this bleak great shed, full of Fleetwood Mac equipment in boxes with little wheels, we sit and talk through the show. A couple of short songs from the album are to go in – 'Sit On My Face' at the start of Part II and Terry's 'Never Be Rude to an Arab' (though Terry does very much want to do his Scottish poem about the otter – this doesn't impress overmuch, thought he audi-tions it courageously). John and Eric are doing 'Pope and Michelangelo' instead of 'Secret Service' and one of TG's anima-tions – 'History of Flight' – may be cut.

Afternoon spent running words – and making ourselves laugh as we renew acquaintance with the show and material we haven't done together for over four years. In particular 'Salvation Fuzz' – perhaps the most anarchic and unruly and disorderly of all the sketches – gets us going. A very heartening afternoon.

Monday, September 22nd, Los Angeles

To rehearsal at 10.30. André is there, and also Mollie Kirkland – the very efficient stage manager, who worked on the City Center[1] show. Both welcome and reassuring faces.

Apart from two thoroughly enjoyable runthroughs in our rehearsal cavern, there seems to be little really good news about the shows. Ticket sales are only at 50% so far.

We are all concentrating on tightening, sharpening and adding to the show. And in this we have been successful – our approach and our spirit is much less tense than it was in New York.

Tuesday, September 23rd, Los Angeles

John said he never wanted to repeat the thirteen weeks of what he considers non-productivity on the script this year. It was history repeating itself, 1972 all over again.

A mood of determined resolution not to be brought down by John's despondency grows. TG, away from so much of the Python

---

1. *Monty Python Live at City Center*, New York, 1976.

meetings this year, is here, and Graham joins us too, and we reaffirm a basic aspect of our work together, which JC and Denis O'B and others sometimes tend to cloud, which is that it's fun.

Wednesday, September 24th, Los Angeles

Drive myself up to the Bowl. Still the rig has not been finished. Neither of the twenty-foot-high eidophor screens are up, but otherwise, with drapes now hung, the acting area is beginning to feel and look quite intimate.

Friday, September 26th, Los Angeles

Back at the Bowl, five thousand paying customers. Denis has had to drop the lowest price from ten dollars to seven to try and fill up the extra seats. So there are about five-and-a-half thousand folk out there for opening night.

The show goes well. The audience is reassuringly noisy, familiar, ecstatic as they hear their favourite sketches announced – and it's as if we had never been away. A continuation of the best of our City Center shows.

Sunday, September 28th, Los Angeles

GC's book *Autobiography of a Liar* [in fact it was called *A Liar's Autobiography*] has been one of the features of this trip. Coming out at the same time as Roger Wilmut's 'History of Python' [*From Fringe to Flying Circus*] – which is straight and competent and almost depressingly like an early obituary – GC's is a sharp, funny, chaotic, wild, touching and extraordinary book. Written in great style, very lively, it's already got TJ very angry about misrepresentation and JC greatly relieved, for some reason, that it doesn't say unpleasant things about him.

Monday, September 29th, Los Angeles

Anne reckons our BO take over the four nights will be $350,000 – the total possible being $450,000. Not a crashing success, but we'll cover costs. Any revenue will come from the TV sales, which Denis says will only fetch $300,000. There are, however, the invisible earnings that it's impossible to quantify – record sales, movie rerun attendances, and just keeping the Python name up front there.

Wednesday, October 8th

Rather staid interview with the BBC at Broadcasting House. TJ does it with me.

The IBA [Independent Broadcasting Authority] ban on TV or radio advertising of *Monty Python's Contractual Obligation* provides the main gist of the chat.

'Do *you* think it's filth?' she asks us.

'Oh, yes,' we reply hopefully... and I add 'and worse than that, puerile filth...'

The nice lady interviewer doesn't know quite what to make of a comedy album called *Monty Python's Contractual Obligation* and neither do we. But all parties try hard.

Thursday, October 23rd

J Goldstone rings to say that the *Life of Brian* appears to be making great progress in Barcelona. Starting slowly, it got good reviews, and after two or three days audiences began to pour in.

Monday, November 3rd

First meeting of Pythons Without John for Further Work on the New Film.

Anne has, I gather on Eric's instigation, kitted out the downstairs room of 2 Park Square West as a Python writing place. We have a table and our own coffee machine and some flowers thoughtfully laid out on top of a filing cabinet.

Tuesday, November 4th

Life of Brian, after much censorship to-ing and fro-ing, finally opened in Norway last week and has taken $100,000 in the first three days. And in Australia the album has sold 25,000 copies in a couple of weeks and is now officially a gold album there.

Thursday, November 20th

Into the Python meeting at 10.30.

At 12.30, J Cleese arrives to play with the Space Invaders game and watch the sixty-minute video of the Hollywood Bowl stage show – which JC has been in charge of editing. All of us feel the sense of occasion is lacking. It is, after all, *Python Live at the Hollywood Bowl* and at the moment it's just Python Live Against Black Drapes. TJ's initial worry that it would look boring is borne out.

Should there be a possible eighty-three-minute version for theatrical viewing? TJ and EI feel emphatically no, the rest of us would like to see one assembled. I feel that if the material is well done (and performances at the Bowl weren't bad) and the cartoon film sequences are fresh, we could quite honourably sell it in France, Scandinavia, Australia and possibly Canada at least.

Friday, November 28th

A successful readthrough. Eric has written a classic – 'The Liberal Family'.

Tuesday, December 2nd

Today we sit and stare at the board on the wall on which cards bearing the names of sketches have been hopefully pinned. Graham muses rather distantly, and Terry and I sputter on. But around lunchtime it dies. We only have a working lunch – sandwiches on the table – and afterwards Eric, who has been in one of his silent spells, suddenly galvanises us all into working out a story.

The end of the world, 6000 AD, the bomber with the Ultimate Weapon, all disappear and we build on the one constant of the month – the working-class family sketch of mine, a fabric of a story about – guess what? – three brothers of the Forbes-Bayter family and the rise to fame, wealth and power of Trevor from obscure working-class origins to become Prime Minister just as the final nuclear war breaks out.

I can hardly believe that after all this work and discussion we have come around to a 'Ripping Yarn' which Terry and I could have written in a fortnight on our own.

Wednesday, December 3rd

I have to say as we meet that I do think the family story we worked out yesterday was a soft option and that the End of the World and the ninety-minute countdown remains for me a much more striking idea and a more thoughtful subject altogether. There is no disagreement here and for a while it seems that we have two films. A 'Yarn' and an 'Apocalypse'. Terry J loves the idea of making two films at the same time and showing them at cinemas on alternate nights – Monty Python's two new films.

Friday, December 5th

To EuroAtlantic for the six o'clock Python meeting. Denis O'B has stage-managed the encounter quite carefully. There is an air of calculated informality.

Then one by one the various members of the EuroAtlantic team give us a report – which sounds less like a report and more like a justification, at times as blatant as a sales pitch, of their own usefulness. Even though John Cleese isn't present they still sound intimidated, and there is an unrelaxed air to the proceedings until Steve Abbott[1] punctures it well.

The atmosphere is very different from the unalloyed enthusiasm of the New Dawn of Python beside the swimming pool at Fisher's Island fourteen months ago.

I drive Anne back at the end of the meeting and she is fuming.

Monday, March 30th, 1981

Drive down to the first of a week's Python meetings at 2 Park Square West.

We appear to be very much in accord over our exasperation, frustration and consternation about Denis's role in our affairs. In Anne's painstakingly assembled report on life with EuroAtlantic, she suggested that she and Steve (Abbott) could run our day-to-day affairs from 2 PSW.

---

1. A bright young Bradford-born accountant, not long down from Cambridge and recently employed by Denis O'Brien's company, EuroAtlantic, in Cadogan Square, Knightsbridge.

A remarkable degree of unanimity within the group that now is the time to sort out this whole question.

Wednesday, April 1st

A dry, warm day with soft, high cloud. Everyone in a good mood. Eric suggests we all of us make a list of the pros and cons of D O'B. The lists turn out to be remarkably similar. Tax planning and tax structures are commended, but all the pro lists are much shorter than the cons – which include over-secrecy, inability to listen to or understand things he doesn't want to hear, and use of the word 'philosophy'.

Friday, April 3rd

Denis is pleased that we have decided to go ahead with theatrical release of *Hollywood Bowl*. Which we now decide to call, simply, *Monty Python at the Hollywood Bowl*. But try as we can to drill into him that he should go for smaller distributors with more time to listen, the more Denis retreats back to the majors whom he knows.

Monday, April 6th

It's quite obvious that the group as a whole trust Anne more than Denis (JC wanted it to go on record that he mistrusted Denis less than the rest of us), and Eric was the only one who signed the letter to Denis with his surname. 'Denis is the sort of person I want to be on surname terms with,' was the way he put it – and I promised to write that in my diary.

Monday, April 13th

Help prepare for dinner with Steve Abbott and friend Laurie.

Part of my reason for asking him round is to find out more about his feelings about Denis and Euro. Basically he is concerned about divided loyalties. He cannot carry on working for the Pythons and doing what is best for the Pythons within the EuroAtlantic framework because he feels the decisions taken for the benefit of EuroAtlantic are very often contrary to the benefit of the Pythons.

Steve is, I think, a man of good, basic, honest convictions, and if for this reason he's leaving EuroAtlantic, it makes me listen very carefully.

Sunday, April 19th, Southwold, Easter Sunday

In the afternoon I read through Robert [Hewison]'s manuscript of the Python censorship book [*Irreverence, scurrility, profanity, vilification and licentious abuse: Monty Python the Case Against*]. It's well researched, thorough, lightly, but not uncritically, biased in our favour. The word I've written in my notes to sum up his endeavour is 'scrupulous'. It's really everything I hoped it would be.

Saturday, May 2nd, London to The Chewton Glen Hotel

Drive down to Hampshire for the Python weekend.

The Chewton Glen Hotel is unashamedly expensive. But it suits our purposes – we're here, after all, to concentrate our minds on one of the most important decisions Python has yet made.

There is remarkably little dissension from JC's opening assessment that we should tell Denis that we no longer feel we need a manager. That there should, in the interests of economy and efficiency, be one Python office to administrate the companies, and that future relationships with Denis should be on an ad hoc basis.

Within a couple of hours we've reached a heartening degree of agreement, and JC is left to compose a letter.

How easily the 'historic' decision has been made. It's not often Python so clearly and unanimously sees the rightness of a decision, and it's such a relief that it's happened like that today. It now remains to be seen how D O'B reacts. I hope he will not see it as a stab in the back, but a stab in the front. He should have seen it coming, and it shouldn't prove fatal.

Sunday, May 3rd

We assemble about 10.15. There's a re-reading of the letter to Denis and some corrections made. JC is so anxious to emphasise our inconstancy that there's a danger the cold reality of the message may not get through.

Then follows a chat about the next film – and one of the remarkable displays of the collective Python mind doing what it does best. Ideas, jokes, themes pour out from everyone round the table so fast that no one wants to stop and write any of them down for fear of losing this glorious impetus. The court framework for the next movie comes up – the idea of us all being hanged for producing a film that is only a tax-dodge. It's all rich and funny and complex and very satisfying.

Tuesday, May 5th

Work on the script – slowly but surely. Anne comes round at lunchtime with the letter to Denis to sign. JC has put back some of the wordiness that Eric and I took out, but it seems to be clear and bending over backwards to give us the blame!

Friday, May 8th

Denis rings. He's back and he has evidently seen the Chewton Glen letter.

He sounded calm, and in a realistic frame of mind. He was not entirely clear about what the letter proposed – could I elucidate? I elucidated as best I could. We wanted D O'B to be an ad hoc, independent figure who we could come to for the major things he'd proved himself good at. Our essential aim was to simplify our business affairs.

D O'B was silent for a moment, but seemed to accept all this.

Monday, May 11th

A meeting with Denis O'B. I [was] the last to arrive (apart from Eric, who was just then landing in New York). At about 7.20, after we'd been talking for an hour, John had to leave. So it was left to the four of us to decide on the next move with Denis.

Was there an alternative to complete and final termination? Terry J asked. Denis didn't like this. It was all or nothing. He wanted to be free to concentrate on all the other areas EuroAtlantic could go in. He might, he said, get out of films altogether.

So at about eight o'clock, as a dull evening was drawing to a close outside, we had to take a decision. Should we terminate? It really was the only answer. It was what the letter, signed by us all on May 5th, had said anyway.

Friday, May 22nd

This is the day appointed for the changeover of Python affairs from EuroAtlantic at 26 Cadogan Square back to the more leisurely Nash terraces of Regent's Park. From today Steve and Lena (Granstedt, his assistant) work for Python and not EA.

Friday, June 5th

Drive up to 2 Park Square West for a Python meeting.

There is a long agenda, and yet we spend the first half-hour talking about possible changes to the Hollywood Bowl film. John is quite despairing. He buries his head in his hands and summons up what appear to be his very last resources of patience. 'I crave order,' he groans, looking at the remnants of the agenda, whilst Terry J suggests we put Neil [Innes] in the film and possibly a bit more animation, and JC moans inwardly that he only wants to do this 'bloody thing' to make some money (I rather agree), and Eric it is who puts the frustrating but incontrovertible arguments for protecting our reputation by putting out only what we think is the best.

Thursday, July 16th

Drove on down to Terry J's. Terry is on good form. Realise that I'm enjoying writing with an immediate sounding board again. In fact I have rather a good day and add to the 'Catholic Family' sketch rather satisfactorily.

The final twelve months of work on
writing *The Meaning of Life*,
in between work on other projects
involving the Pythons as individuals
(July 1981–July 1982)

1981–1982

Monday, July 20th

Start of a Python writing fortnight. We tried such a session a year ago, and it was not successful. Today, a year later, things feel very different.

Time Bandits is complete, so TG is back with the group. Graham, with *Yellowbeard*, and myself, with *The Missionary*, both have projects which look like being completed by summer '82.

We decided, without any bickering or grudging, that we should now work separately until the end of the week.

Monday, July 27th

A successful day, everyone participating. John tending to chair in a barristerish way, but it's all good Python trough work. We re-read the 'Bankers'. They nearly all survive, and, by half past three when TJ has to go, we have a solid fifty minutes, with viable links and a sort of coherence.

Thursday, September 3rd

Viewing of *Hollywood Bowl* on screen for first time. Sixty-five minutes it runs. Sketches well performed and quite well filmed – the rest a wretched disappointment.

Back at Neal's Yard, those Pythons who saw the film – Terry J, John, Graham and myself (TG and Eric being in France) – all agree it isn't right. Main criticisms – links, atmosphere, shapelessness.

I felt very proud of our little group today. In the face of much pressure to put the *Bowl* film out as soon as possible, to recoup our money and to have done with it, we held out for quality control first.

Wednesday, November 25th

To Park Square West for Python writing.

We proceed well on a general pattern and order of sketches. But at one point the Oxford/Cambridge split, avoided most successfully for the rest of this week, suddenly gapes. The point on which we argue is not a major one, but John rationalises his obstinacy as being the result of his grasp of 'the structure'. It's hard work, but in the end he wins his point.

Tuesday, December 1st

Into Python meeting at 10.30. I read the large chunk that TJ and I have put together right from the start to beyond 'Middle of the Film' and into the 'randy' sequence – which goes exceptionally well. The whole lot is very well received and even applauded.

JC and GC have written some first-class stuff about an Ayatollah, but then one or two of their later scenes – especially a torture sequence – drags on and becomes a bore. Eric has written a couple of nice things and plays us a song he's recorded – 'Christmas in Heaven'.

Wednesday, December 2nd

TJ arrives at 1.30. Unfortunately only a small part of the section I'm rather proud of makes TJ laugh, so we ditch most of it and, in the two-and-a-half hours remaining, cobble together a possible penultimate sequence, starting with the Ayatollah breaking into the sex lecture and the firing squad of menstruating women. It's mainly TJ's work.

Saturday, January 9th, 1982

A viewing of the *Hollywood Bowl* film – the first since Julian (Doyle) spent weeks trying to lick it into shape in LA. And it is greatly improved – linked far more smoothly and the sense of live occasion much stronger now there are better-chosen cut-backs to audience, etc. In short, a film which we now feel we will not be ashamed of. Performances very strong, particularly Eric.

It had been decided that, as with Life of Brian *and* Barbados, *we needed somewhere exotic to finalise the new film script; Jamaica had been chosen.*

Sunday, January 10th, Jamaica

Touch down in Montego Bay about 8.30. A large black limousine is backed up outside and Brian, our driver (why is there always a Brian wherever Python goes?) squeezes us all and luggage in. We turn into the drive of a long, low, unadorned rectangular mansion, called Unity, some time after ten o'clock. A youngish black man, Winford, and a middle-aged, beaming black lady, Beryl, come out to settle us in.

Winford advises us not to swim tonight as there are barracuda which come in from behind the reef at night-time. But it's a lovely night with a big full moon.

Monday, January 11th, Runaway Bay, Jamaica

Everyone's reactions to the script are discussed. All of us, to some extent, feel disappointed. I think the material is still very static. It could still be a radio show.

It's agreed that we should proceed from the material we have and create a strong story or framework to contain it. Some silly moments in this free and fairly relaxed session – including a title from TG, 'Jesus's Revenge'. But though everyone occasionally flashes and sparkles, nothing ignites.

Wednesday, January 13th, Jamaica

An early breakfast, and splitting into groups by 9.30. Terry J and Terry G, Eric and JC, myself and Graham.

GC and I, however, soon find ourselves in one of the most bizarre and distracted writing sessions of all time. Beryl, the cook, was under the impression that someone would take her up to the market, eight miles away, for all the provisions she will need for the

Jamaican food we've asked her to produce. So GC and I decide to take her and work on the way.

It starts quite well as we drive up winding mountain roads for a half-hour and emerge into a busy little township. GC and I make a quick shopping sortie for shoes and swimming trunks then back to the car. Vegetables in the back, but no Beryl.

Still talking over our idea for a John Buchan-type story framework, we have a Red Stripe beer in a small bar. Beryl comes back and deposits fish, but then has to sally back into the market for yams. Stop at the supermarket for bully beef, and our writing session finally turns into the gates of Unity two-and-a-half hours after we set out.

After lunch we sit and present our ideas. I present GC's and mine. A breathtaking, marvellously choreographed musical overture all about fish – with us in spectacular fishy costumes. Then into an exciting Buchan mystery tale, involving strange disappearances, unexplained deaths, all pointing to Kashmir.

The hero would have to unravel the story by various clues, which bring in our existing sketches.

John and Eric have taken the view that the film is primarily about sex and they've reinstated the Janine/girls' paradise idea that I'd gone off a year ago. Even less response to this idea.

TG and TJ have gone back to first Python principles to link it – a ragbag of non sequiturs and complex connections. It's full and frantic and, when TJ's finished describing it, there is silence. It's as if no one can really cope with any more 'solutions'. As if this is the moment that this material – the best of three years' writing – finally defeated us.

Thursday, January 14th, Jamaica

Wake to sunshine and a feeling that today is make-or-break for the film. We certainly cannot continue stumbling into the darkness as we did yesterday.

TJ says that, from the timings of the sketches we all like alone, we have over 100 minutes of material. This seems to spur people into another effort. TJ suggests a trilogy. The idea of a rather pretentious Three Ages of Man comes up and a title 'Monty Python's Meaning of Life', to which Eric adds the subhead 'See it now! Before it's out of date'.

We decide to group the material together into phoney pseudo-scientific headings – 'Birth', 'Fighting Each Other' and 'Death'. Suddenly ideas come spilling out and within an hour there seems to be a remarkable change in the film's fortunes.

Friday, January 15th, Jamaica

Writing has definitely taken a turn for the better. Eric, TJ and I in the big room make some encouraging progress on linking the 'War/Fighting Each Other' section.

Saturday, January 16th, Jamaica

Set to with Eric and TJ to put the last section of *The Meaning of Life* into shape.

At 4.30 everyone returns to read through work assembled over the last three days. JC and GC and TG have come up with a tremendously good, strong opening set in a hospital during the birth of a child, and there is only one section of the film about which people have doubts.

The *Meaning of Life* theme and structure does seem to have saved the film, and justified our being here. There are now tightenings and improvements to be done and songs to be written, and these will occupy us for our four remaining writing days.

Thursday, January 20th, Jamaica

There isn't a lot to do but type up. It's decided to meet in London for three days in mid-February and then to take a final decision on whether to go ahead.

No one, I think, feels we have a *Brian* on our hands, but there is a hope that we have something which we all feel we could film in the summer.

Monday, February 15th

Terry G rings spluttering with uncontrollable laughter. He had just finished reading 'Mr Creosote' and had to tell someone how near to jelly it had reduced him.

Monday, March 22nd

A long Python film meeting.

The apportionment of parts, which took us a couple of very good-humoured hours after lunch, is such an important moment in the creation of the film; we've been writing for three-and-a-half years, and yet the impact of the movie for audiences is probably far more affected by what happened in the seventy-five minutes at Park Square West this afternoon.

I don't think there are any rank sores or festering injustices, though TJ thinks Eric may have wanted to do the end song ['Christmas in Heaven'], which has gone to Graham – doing a Tony Bennett impersonation!

Universal have few qualms about giving us the money – three million dollars up front, assuring us each of over £150,000 by the end of the year, well before the movie goes out. Python has never had better terms. [Despite earlier interest from Paramount and Warners, the film was made by Universal.]

Sunday, May 16th

TJ rings. He says he reckons doing *Meaning of Life* will be a doddle. I gather Peter Hannan has been sent a script and is first choice for cameraman.

Monday, June 28th

The start of Python rehearsals and writing for *Meaning of Life*. *Python Live at the Hollywood Bowl* opened at sixty to seventy cinemas in NYC and Philadelphia to overwhelming apathy. Various reasons put forward.

After a half-hour discussion it's clear that no one has an answer. The movie collected good reviews in both the big NYC papers.

Eric wins 'The Meaning of Life' song with no declared supporters for TJ's version apart from myself and TG, and neither of us felt Eric's version deserving of any stick. But on 'Every Sperm is Sacred', on which TJ has done – *had* to do – so much work, there is quite a strong split. Eric takes up the position that his version is much better, musically and in every other way, than TJ's. GC bears him out quite vehemently. TJ says that his version is better, musically and in every other way, than Eric's.

Once we start discussion it's clearly crucial that JC comes down firmly in favour of TJ's version.

Tuesday, June 29th

Sandwiches at lunch and talk over the ending. Eric feels that we have cheated the audience by not having come to grips with our title. I see our title as being a statement in itself. There is no way we can tell anyone the meaning of life – it's a cliché and we are using it ironically to show how irrelevant we can be when faced with such a pretentious subject. John sees fish as the answer to our problem.

Eventually I ad-lib, with Eric's help, a very short and dismissive lady presenter winding up the film and reading the meaning of life from an envelope – this fed on from a nice idea of a Hollywood awards-type ceremony where we asked a glittery compère to come on and reveal the meaning of life. He opens a gold envelope and reads... 'And the meaning of life is... Colin Welland!' I think this was the best laugh of the day.[1]

1. At the 1982 Academy Awards, Welland had famously brandished the Oscar for *Chariots of Fire* and shouted 'The British Are Coming!'

21

Filming *The Meaning of Life*
(July–September 1982)

1982

Thursday, July 8th

To the Royal Masonic School in Bushey, a largely red-brick amalgam of all the old public-school architectural clichés. A few flying buttresses here, a clock tower and some cloisters there.

We're starting with a scene involving Cleese and myself and an entire chapelful of boys and masters. I play a chaplain.

Friday, July 23rd

This morning I am spurred on by the sight of light at the end of the tunnel – by the prospect of not only a weekend off, but then seven filming days in which I'm not involved.

But today is no easy downhill slope. For a start, Eric and I have a long dialogue scene (in the hotel sequence) – four-and-a-half minutes or so. TG has a wonderfully complex and grotesque make-up as the Arab Porter. Then there is much relighting and building of rostrums after TJ decides to shoot the whole scene in one. So Eric and I walk through at 8.30, then wait, in make-up and costume, until a quarter to one before they are ready.

We do two or three takes at about 1.30, and in two of them I forget my lines and have to stop – which is unusual enough for me to make me rather cross and depressed when lunchtime comes. Fortunately, after lunch with EI and the strangely attired Gilliam, I feel better and, although I have to push myself physically hard, I find that I'm actually enjoying the piece.

TG, with his blind eye (as used in *Holy Grail*), nose too big for him and the wheel on his false hand broken, has created for himself his own peculiar nightmare, and he will be trapped in it again on Monday.

Monday, July 26th

With the lighting already up and the Hendy hotel-room piece already played through, I'm ready for my close-ups by a quarter to nine and have done the scene by 9.30. I feel looser and funnier and much more on top of the scene than last Friday and almost wish we could do the whole thing again.

But Eric is much quieter today. He apparently suffered a twenty-four-hour flu yesterday, with hallucinations and temperature. His voice is huskier than Friday, and he is clearly not happy with the performance. But he improves as we go on, and cheers up too.

Tuesday, August 3rd

See assembly of 'Mr Creosote' at lunchtime (instead of lunch). Evidently 9,000 gallons of vomit were made for the sketch, which took four days to film. It's been edited rather loosely at a poor pace and dwelling too much on TJ's actual vomiting, but the costume is marvellous in its enormous surreal bulk, and Mr C's explosion is quite awful and splendid.

Thursday, August 5th

Collected at 8.30 by Brian. I have a one-hour make-up as Debbie Katzenburg.

Eric, TJ and myself in drag, Cleese the Reaper, Chapman and TG the men. One of the few sketches involving all the Pythons.

The afternoon's work is slow – things like JC's beckoning bony finger taking up a lot of time, as special effects, animals and children always do.

Friday, August 6th

A long morning around the table in a hot studio in drag. Simon Jones is playing the sixth member of the dinner party. He's a very good man with a quiet wit, well able to stand up for himself. In one morning he learnt the Python lesson in survival – overact in your close-up, it's your only chance. Actually he did his piece modestly and very well.

Long afternoon as we have to dress in cottage walls [i.e. bring the walls in as background] every time we move round to do close-ups. GC and I are the last to be done. Then more special effects as we die. Eric and I blow out the candles then collapse, motionless on the table for forty seconds. Cynthia Cleese hiccups during one of these long silences and sets us all off.

Saturday, August 7th

Up to Elstree for a tiger-skin fitting, only to find that my other half of the skin is in a pink suit doing the 'Galaxy Song' on Stage 3. Yet another breakdown in communication. Round to Stage 4 where mighty office buildings are being erected for TG's £100,000 'Accountancy/Pirate' epic.

Tucked in a corner is a tiny Yorkshire thirties cottage, filled with children who are rehearsing 'Every Sperm' for Monday. Little Arlene Phillips, with her bright, open face and pink and maroon matching hair and tracksuit, is taking the kids through the number. We work out some movements for me to do, and then I read the build-up lines – all about 'Little rubber things on the end of me cock' – some kids snigger, the younger ones smile up at me innocently.

Tuesday, August 10th

Arrive at Elstree 9.15. Wide shots first, with all the kids in. Mothers in attendance.

TJ is worried that there may be a walk-out if we say either my line – 'Little rubber thing on the end of my cock' – or one of the kids' lines – 'Couldn't you have your balls cut off?' – so we plan a subterfuge. I will say 'sock' instead of 'cock' (taking care not to overemphasise the initial letter) and then the dastardly substitution will take place in the dubbing theatre. The boy's interruption will be of a quite harmless variety – 'Couldn't you sell Mother for scrap?' – when everyone is present, but we'll record the real line separately when everyone's gone.

The afternoon is very hard work. I have to go through the opening speeches, song and routine over and over and the room is warming up, and the kids, though well behaved, have to be continually instructed and calmed down, which gets tiring.

Finish with the children (as we have to by law) at 5.30, and for a moment Ray Corbett (first assistant director), Hannan [cameraman], Terry, Dewi[1] and myself slump onto chairs in the little room amongst the discarded toys – like shattered parents at the end of a two-day children's party. Then, with a supreme effort, we gird our loins and complete my tight close-ups. I end the day wild-tracking the phrase 'Little rubber thing on the end of my cock'... 'over the end of my cock', and so on.

Thursday, August 12th, Glasgow

Leave the hotel at 8.30. Drive half an hour out to the north of the city. Then through wooded, pleasant suburbs to Strathbone, where we are quartered.

Some hanging around, talking to local press, crossword-puzzling and finally making up with mutton-chop whiskers and moustache, and squeezing into custom-made leather boots and the rather handsome navy-blue uniform of a major in the Warwickshires of 1879.

Then we're driven a mile to the location – a five-minute walk up a hillside, where a British encampment has been constructed beneath a bare rock cliff, which I later gather is known in the area as Jennie's Lump.

Sudden drenching squalls of rain and cold wind cause us to abandon the planned shots and spend the day on weather-cover, with scenes inside the tent originally planned for Elstree. But it isn't only the unsettled weather which is forcing us to use weather-cover. Rumour reaches us during the morning that nearly 100 of our carefully selected and measured Glaswegian extras have walked out after a misunderstanding over costume in the local village hall.

A small group of very vocal Africans became angry when they were shown how to tie loincloths by Jim Acheson.[2] They had been misled, they shouted. They thought they would be wearing suits.

---

1. Dewi Humphreys, camera operator, went on to become a successful TV director (*Vicar of Dibley*, *Absolutely Fabulous* and many more).
2. Acheson later won three Oscars for Costume Design: *The Last Emperor* (1987), *Dangerous Liaisons* (1988) and *Restoration* (1995).

Poor Jim and his excellent wardrobe team faced a 1982 Zulu Uprising, as a group of two or three blacks shouted about being degraded, tricked... dishonoured, etc., etc.... And 100 of them were taken back in buses to Glasgow.

We went on shooting – oblivious to all this – and completed most of the tent interiors by six o'clock.

Friday, August 13th, Glasgow

We have had to recruit white Glaswegians and brown them up as Zulus. I must say they are very patient and charge at the encampment ten times. It's a long day, heavy on extras and blood and smoke, and light on lines for the officers.

Newspapers – local and national – carry the story of the Zulus yesterday. Some very funny reports, especially in the *Glasgow Herald*.

An extra day's shooting tomorrow.

Monday, August 16th, Bradford and Malham, Yorkshire

Sixth week of Python filming. It looks wet and uninviting outside.

An hour and a half's drive into fine, rugged scenery up on Malham Moors.

Eric, Simon Jones and I wrap ourselves in blankets and wait in an upper room at the hostel. It's an old hunting lodge, which is now a centre for school sixth forms to come for field studies.

Eric and I get into our make-up base for our 'Cocktail Party Ladies'; outside the wind howls and the rain lashes at the windows. God knows what it must be like for Cleese, out on the moors as the Grim Reaper.

JC arrives back at midday, absolutely soaked through, but in surprisingly high spirits. He takes great heart from the fact that TJ thought the shot they'd just done was second only to a day of sea-sickness in the Newhaven lifeboat as the most uncomfortable filming of his life.

Our appearance on the moor is put off well into the afternoon. I organise a subversive but, I feel, necessary, trip to the pub in Malham at lunchtime. As I buy pints of Theakston's, I feel I have to explain to the lady at the bar why I'm in false eyelashes and full ladies' make-up. I tell her I'm in a film. She says apologetically, 'Oh,

I never see films, I'm afraid. If anyone comes in here hoping to be recognised I'm afraid I can't help.'

Friday, August 20th, Bradford

I'm driven out to Skipton at 7.30. A cold wind, occasional rain.

Terry has to ask some householders with strange, lopsided faces if he could throw mud on the walls of their house. 'So long as you don't come *in*side,' they reply fiercely.

Wednesday, August 25th

Because of poor weather this week, the 'Tiger Skin' scene has been postponed and we are doing the 'Hospital' today. Nice to see little Valerie Whittington and Judy Loe again. [Valerie had been in *The Missionary* and Judy in *Ripping Yarns* 'Curse of the Claw']. Valerie has all day with her legs apart as the Mother, Judy is the Nurse. I'm the Hospital Administrator.

Friday, August 27th

We attempt the 'Jungle' scene, so I have two parts to play Pakenham-Walsh and the Rear End of the Tiger.

JC complains about performing against bright lights – quite rightly. It does reduce facial mobility by about 50%. JC mutters bitterly, and not for the first time, about pretty pictures at the expense of performances.

TG, who desperately wants to get this over with, so he can get back to his 'Pirate/Business' epic on Stage 4, is laboriously encased in a complete latex mould of a Zulu. Then the sun goes in, and does not reappear, except for a brief glimpse, when we try the shot. But TG, who's been inside the costume for an hour, has sweated so much that one side of the Zulu sticks to him.

The 'Tiger' is eventually abandoned and instead we shoot the tracking shot of the approach through the forest. Endless takes.

Wednesday, September 8th

To Elstree at lunchtime to be Debbie yet again.

Jonathan Benson is the new first assistant and keeps us all cheered with his special Bensonian brand of dry wit, which comes out, just as does the dry ice, at the beginning of each take.

Saturday, September 11th

Today all the Pythons are together to be fish and, as this is probably the last time we shall be gathered in one place until February next, there is an added note of almost hysterical urgency around. Iain Johnstone's[1] BBC crew are filming the ABC '20-20' film crew filming us trying on our fish harnesses. I'm a goldfish, Graham a grayling, the two Terries perches and John is a carp.

It's a very weird and effective make-up, making us all look like John Tenniel's *Alice* pictures – semi-anthropomorphised.

'Shit, it's Mr Creosote,' are the memorable last words of the day, nine weeks after John and I had begun the film in the chapel of the Royal Masonic School.

1. Iain was a producer and presenter of BBC's *Film Night*. He was also an author and later worked with John Cleese on the book of *A Fish Called Wanda* and the screenplay of *Fierce Creatures*.

Editing and opening *The Meaning of Life*;
a 'family' wedding and the first Python
group meeting for over a year
(December 1982–December 1983)

1982-1983

Sunday, December 26th

Python film viewing at three o'clock. The Bijou is packed and hot and smoky. All sorts of familiar faces there – Eric I conspicuously absent.

The film seems to go very quiet about a third of the way through, but ends very well, with 'Creosote' the high point. Afterwards I find that most people felt the first half worked very satisfactorily and if there *were* any longueurs they were either in the 'Pirate/Accountant' sequence or towards the end. But most people seemed to be quite bowled over by it.

Five out of six Pythons have seen the film. There are no drastic differences of opinion. Everyone feels that TG's 'Pirate/Accountant' section should be in the film, not as a separate little feature on its own. And everyone feels it should be quite heavily pruned. I suggest it should be ten minutes at the most, Terry J about eight, Graham, quite firmly, seven. GC gets a round of applause from the meeting for his performance as Mr Blackitt, and TG for his 'Death' animation.

Thom Mount from Universal, who has come over to discuss release dates, etc., breaks in to announce that he thinks the film is wonderful and he would hardly change a single moment. As he's quite liked and respected by us all, this does visibly change the mood of the discussion.

Universal want some previews in the US as soon as possible to test reaction. They want to attempt a first ad campaign too.

All of which puts considerable pressure on my Indian travelling companion Mr Gilliam, who must cut his 'Pirate' piece, complete his animation and discuss ads, all before he meets me in Delhi on the 23rd of January. [Michael was planning to combine holiday visits to Kenya and India, where he was due to meet Terry Gilliam, with a visit to Australia to publicise *The Missionary*.]

Friday, January 14th, 1983, Adelaide and Sydney

A surprise phone call from Basil Pao, who is in Sydney after three years' 'exile' in Hong Kong. He says he has just received a call from John Goldstone asking if he will design a *Meaning of Life* poster.

No sooner have I put the phone down than Goldstone himself rings to confirm a rumour I heard that Universal want the *Meaning of Life* to open in America at Easter.

Tuesday, February 1st

TJ rings. He's just back from a lightning Concorde trip to the US for *Meaning of Life* previews. Two showings in Yonkers went so badly that TJ and JG didn't even bother to look at the cards [which preview audiences were asked to fill in]. An audience of young (fifteen to twenty-two) cinema-goers predominantly. Eighty walk-outs.

TJ's spirits restored by a showing in Manhattan which was very well received. As often happens under pressure, some sensible cuts have been made quite quickly 'Luther' is gone and much of the 'Hendys' too. The film sounds trimmer. Universal, as a result of these last showings, are definitely going ahead on March 25th, but with a limited release.

Tuesday, March 29th, London–New York

I leave the house to catch the 10.30 Concorde to New York. The flight (all £1,190 of it) to New York is being paid for by Universal Pictures for my work on behalf of the second film I made last year – *The Meaning of Life*. [The first was *The Missionary*.]

Friday, April 1st, New York–London

Down to [an] ABC studio to record an interview with a man whose extravagant name – Regis Philbin – denies his very regular appearance.

We do ten very successful minutes. The producer of this new show is Bob Shanks – the man who six years ago was responsible for the butchering of the six Python TV shows which took us to court, and eventually won us custody of the shows. He looks older and more unkempt. Quite shockingly different from the trim, smooth executive with nary a hair out of place whom we fought at the Federal Courthouse.

He jokes about it as we shake hands. 'We met in court…' Really he's done us a lot of good in the end, and it's a curious coincidence that less than twelve hours before meeting Shanks again, I heard from Ron Devillier that we have sold the Python TV shows to PBS for a fee of at least a million dollars for two years.

Monday, April 25th

On to a Python *MOL* meeting with the two Terrys and John G and Anne. TJ and I put together a nice little forty-second radio ad and it's quite a jolly session. Goldstone says *MOL* is over ten million gross in the US, but we need forty million gross to start making money.

Sunday, May 8th, Cannes

Am met at Nice Côte d'Azur by Duncan Clark, CIC's head of publicity. Terry J arrived yesterday and has already taken all his clothes off and run into the sea for a TV crew.

Monday, May 9th, Cannes

This is Python day at Cannes. We are officially announced – each one introduced – and our answers instantly translated into French. Neither the questions nor the instant translation process make for an easy exchange of information and certainly they don't help our jokes. One woman claims to have been physically ill during 'Creosote'.

Then we are taken up onto the roof and given a photo-grilling of Charles and Di-like proportions, with cameramen fighting each other to get dull pictures of us. I've never, ever been the subject of such concentrated Nikon-ic attention. It's all very silly, and years ago we would all have been persuaded to be much more outrageous.

Then, suddenly, we're free. The Terrys, Graham and Eric go back to the hotel to prepare for the splendours of the Gala Presentation of *MOL* tonight, and me to return to England.

Monday, May 16th

Python's *MOL* is fading. It did well in each area for about three weeks and that was that. It now looks as if it will take less in the US than *Brian* (nine million as against eleven).

Thursday, May 19th

John Goldstone phones at 8 a.m. to tell me that *Meaning of Life* has won second prize at Cannes – the Special Jury Prize.

Monday, June 6th

With not very worthy feelings of guilt, reluctance and resentment, I acknowledge the fact that I could and probably should have spent more time on the *MOL* radio commercials which we're recording this morning.

André's just back from two weeks in California looking more successful every time I see him. JC arrives, GC doesn't.

John looks very hairy with beard and long black hair. He is in quite a skittish mood and wants to do lots of silly voices. He does an excellent Kierkegaard.

Wednesday, October 5th

Barry Took is very agitated about *The Meaning of Life*. His attack is rambling but persistent. Badly shot, disgustingly unfunny – back to 'the urine-drinking' aspect of Python, he thundered. All in all, from an old friend, a strange and manic performance.

Saturday, December 3rd

To St Paul's, Covent Garden, for Nancy [Lewis] and Simon [Jones's] wedding.

A heavily bearded Eric Idle slips into the row next to me. What an extraordinary place for a Python reunion. A year after making our second 'blasphemous' comedy, we're in a church singing 'Love Divine All Loves Excelling'.

Cleese, alone, is two rows in front. He keeps making Dick Vosburgh laugh by singing with great emphasis words like 'next', long after everyone else has stopped. Gilliam, with family, is in the front. Terry has his duvet-like coat and, with his new, short haircut, Eric says he looks like an 'inflated monk'. Jones, also with family, has a mac that makes him look like Jones of the Yard, and, entirely suitably, Graham is late!

Someone has alerted the press and there is a barrage of photographers, who try to get all the Pythons to link arms with the bride and groom. John and Graham totally ignore them. But eventually, after persuasive lines like 'Two minutes and we'll leave you alone', we are snapped and can go back to reacquainting ourselves with those we haven't seen for far too long.

Tuesday, December 6th

André rings us to tell me the good news that our *Meaning of Life* commercials have won Best Use of Comedy on a Commercial and Best Entertainment at the Radio Awards. The entire series of commercials received a commendation. André very chuffed. When I think that we threw together the scripts almost on the spot, it's even more remarkable.

Sunday, December 18th

Leave the house at 10.15 for a Python group meeting – the first for over a year.

The meeting is good-natured. Arthur Young, McClelland Moores' accounts are not only accepted and the accountants reappointed but, at TG's suggestion, a motion is passed that a singing telegram should be sent round to tell them so.

Graham asks if he can vote by proxy and if so can he be his own proxy. John Cleese reveals that he may be Jewish. He also says his father had a nanny who had been kissed by Napoleon. I tell them that my ancestor had hidden Prince Charles in the oak tree after the battle of Worcester. To which EI came up with the O-level Maths question 'How many royalists does it require to hide a king in an oak tree?' Graham says he's discovered family links with George Eliot.

*

[Although individual members of Monty Python would frequently work together in later films and live performances, *The Meaning of Life* was the last collaboration involving all six of them. Graham Chapman died in 1989. In 2013, the five remaining Pythons announced that they would perform a new stage show in July 2014.]

EPILOGUE
Michael Palin

For a long time it seemed that *The Meaning of Life* was the end of the road for Python. Its long gestation and unsensational performance at the box office seemed to suggest that it was time to put it all to bed. The award of the Grand Prix de Jury at Cannes appeared to indicate that our future lay more in the cosy boudoir of critical recognition rather than the sunlit uplands of commercial fervour.

We saw the signs and went our own ways, taking comfort from the fact that Python had had a pretty good run. There was no precedent for a groundbreaking TV comedy team morphing into a groundbreaking movie-making business. But two things brought us back together. One was the continuing appetite for Python. If we weren't going to produce any new work then loyal fans, and there were many, would run and rerun the work we had already produced. They did this so successfully that by the 1990s a whole generation of fans were teaching their kids about it and the kids were as amused by it all as their parents. As a result, the funds kept coming in and that involved the business meetings which we all hated but which kept us all talking to each other. And as only Pythons could talk about what it was like to be a Python, we realised that we had something between us that couldn't be put away and forgotten. Eric came up with the idea of *Spamalot*. After a certain amount of huffing and puffing the rest of us endorsed it and, lo and behold, Python was given a new lease of life. In 2012, a niggly legal action about merchandising rights to Python, brought on by the success of *Spamalot*, was the first of our three court appearances not to go entirely our way. A big business meeting in the autumn of 2013 led to a big decision. That we should get together one more time. Forty-five years on from our first public appearance in October 1969, we agreed to bring out the soft cushions and the dead parrots at a concert at the O2 Arena in London. If we sold all the tickets we'd be prepared to do another. At the time of writing, ten stage shows are now planned for July 2014.

London, January 2014

A BASIC CHRONOLOGY
1969–1983

Titles and transmission dates of TV series, titles and release dates of films, titles and publication dates of books, titles and release dates of record albums.

Television Series

Three series of *Monty Python's Flying Circus*

First series: 13 programmes transmitted between 5 October 1969 and 11 January 1970

Second series: 13 programmes transmitted between 15 September 1970 and 22 December 1970

Third series: 13 programmes transmitted between 19 October 1972 and 18 January 1973

Fourth series: *Monty Python* 6 programmes transmitted between 31 October 1974 and 5 December 1974. 'The Golden Age of Ballooning', 'Michael Ellis', 'Light Entertainment War', 'Hamlet', 'Mr Neutron', 'Party Political Broadcast'

Films

And Now for Something Completely Different   1971

Monty Python and the Holy Grail   1975

Monty Python's Life of Brian   1979

Monty Python Live at the Hollywood Bowl   1982

Monty Python's The Meaning of Life   1983

Record Albums

Monty Python's Flying Circus   1970

Another Monty Python Record   1971

Monty Python's Previous Record   1972

The Monty Python Matching Tie and Handkerchief   1973

Monty Python Live at Drury Lane   1974

Monty Python and the Holy Grail   1975

Monty Python Live at City Center   1976

The Monty Python Instant Record Collection   1977

Monty Python's Life of Brian   1979

Monty Python's Contractual Obligation Album   1980

Books

Monty Python's Big Red Book   1971

The Brand New Monty Python Bok   1973

The Brand New Monty Python Papperbok (paperback edition) 1974

Monty Python and the Holy Grail (Book)   1977

Monty Python: Life of Brian/Montypythonscrapbook   1979

Monty Python's The Meaning of Life   1983

www.nickhernbooks.co.uk

 facebook.com/nickhernbooks

 twitter.com/nickhernbooks